PROGRESSIVE CAPITALISM

PROGRESSIVE CAPITALISM

*How to Achieve Economic Growth,
Liberty and Social Justice*

David Sainsbury

Biteback Publishing

First published in Great Britain in 2013 by
Biteback Publishing Ltd
Westminster Tower
3 Albert Embankment
London SE1 7SP
Copyright © David Sainsbury 2013

ISBN 978-1-84954-529-7

10 9 8 7 6 5 4 3 2 1

A CIP catalogue record for this book is available from the British Library.

Set in Perpetua

Printed and bound in Great Britain by
CPI Group (UK) Ltd, Croydon CR0 4YY

To my wife Susie and my daughters Clare, Lucy and Francesca, who share the values on which this book is based, and without whose loving support this book would not have been written.

The present state of the nations is the result of the accumulation of all discoveries, inventions, improvements, perfections and exertions of all generations which have lived before us: they form the mental capital of the present human race, and every separate nation is productive only in the proportion in which it has known how to appropriate these attainments of former generations and to increase them by its own acquirements.

— Friedrich List (1841) *The National System of Political Economy*

CONTENTS

PREFACE

When in 1998 I became Minister of Science and Innovation in the Department of Trade and Industry in Tony Blair's Labour government, I believed the policies we had developed in opposition would increase the prosperity of the country and create a fairer society. But in government I gradually came to realise that our thinking largely reflected the dominant neo-liberal political economy of the time, which was not a useful basis for developing policies to achieve our goals. Across the government there was also a lack of understanding about the nature of economic growth and competition in the global economy, and science and innovation were seen as of marginal importance.

In the field of science and innovation, with the enthusiastic support of Gordon Brown, I think we made some important and useful reforms, as well as greatly increasing the funds for research and knowledge transfer. But it was on too small a scale, and I have no doubt we could have had a larger impact if, before coming into government, we had developed a Progressive political economy which provided us with a more realistic model of capitalism for policy-making purposes. We would also have stood a better chance of seeing the institutional failures that were gradually developing in financial markets. In retrospect, however, it is not surprising we didn't develop such a Progressive political economy because to do so would have meant going against the whole tide of economic thinking at the time.

During my time in government I also became increasingly aware, as a result of many trips to China, Taiwan and South Korea, of the challenge that Western governments were beginning to face as a result of globalisation, the fast growth of the countries of Asia, and the fact that, as a result of the collapse of Communism in Russia, China's shift to market capitalism and India's dismantling of its command-and-control economy, 1.5 billion more low-paid workers had entered the world's labour market.

It was only after I had left government after eight years, however, that I began to question fundamentally the neo-liberal political economy which had dominated the economic policies of governments in the Western world for the last thirty-five years, and form the view that if as a country we were going to rise to the challenge of restructuring our economy to meet the dynamic changes taking place across the world, we would need a new Progressive political economy. This would need to be based on a better understanding of the process of economic growth, and give a new answer to the central question of political economy: what is the role of government in the economy?

My re-evaluation of the prevailing neo-liberal political economy began with a final report on the government's science and technology policies, which I wrote at the request of Gordon Brown, and which I called 'The Race to the Top'. The research for this report strengthened my conviction that there was no way that UK firms could compete with firms in countries like China and India on the basis of price, and that the only way we could compete in the future was on innovation and upgrading the goods and services we sell. We should see ourselves as involved in a 'race to the top', not a 'race to the bottom'. But while the report was enthusiastically supported by Gordon Brown, most politicians and Treasury civil servants seemed unable to take on board the basic message of the report, and this was due to their adherence to neo-liberal ideas.

The second event that greatly affected my thinking was having to fight off a private equity takeover bid for the family business during the summer of 2007. There was not the slightest pretence of seeking to improve the performance of the company, and it was made clear that the current management team, strategy and capital expenditure plans of the business would be kept in place. The only change they proposed to make was to sell off all the properties of the company and replace them with massive debts. Then they would put the company back on the market, stressing the high return on equity but not the high risks involved, and walk away with £1 billion of profit.

This bid, which had the backing of the City, due to the

£100 million of fees the investment banks would earn if it went ahead, seemed to me to be a perfect example of wealth appropriation as opposed to wealth creation, that is to say, it was economic behaviour which aimed to extract value from other participants in the economy without making any contribution to productivity. The bid failed because members of the founding family refused to accept it on the grounds that it would put the future of the business at risk, but the fact that the bid had been made reinforced my view that financial markets were becoming increasingly dysfunctional.

The third event which affected my thinking was, of course, the financial crash of 2008 itself. The coalition government sought to portray it as being the result of the failure of the previous Labour government to control public expenditure. In retrospect the Labour government should have used the opportunity of a strongly growing economy to reduce the deficit, as this would have reduced the pressure on the government to cut back public expenditure at a time when the economy was struggling to lift itself out of a recession. There is a lot to be said for 'fixing the roof when the sun is shining', though I don't remember the Conservative opposition ever making this point when it was shining.

It was also, of course, not the main reason for the financial crash of 2008, which was due to the bursting of a housing bubble accompanied by a massive institutional failure of the financial markets in many parts of the world. The fact that the coalition government, because of its ideological mindset, did not see that there had been a massive failure of the financial markets, and that it was necessary to bring in a major programme of financial reform, hardened my conviction that the neo-liberal political economy, to which they were still clinging, needed to be challenged and a new Progressive political economy put in its place.

I also formed the view that this new Progressive political economy, as well as being based on a better understanding of the process of economic growth, would need to incorporate three defining beliefs of Progressive thinking. The first is the importance of institutions, which can be defined for this purpose as the rules and regulations which society develops so that a specific area of activity functions more effectively.

The second defining belief of Progressive thought concerns the role of the state. Neo-liberals believe that a country's economic institutions start up and evolve spontaneously, but Progressive thinkers believe that the design of institutions involves resolving conflicting interests, and also creates winners and losers, and that an active and competent state has, therefore, to be involved.

And, thirdly, while neo-liberals believe that the performance of an economy should simply be assessed in terms of economic growth and freedom, Progressive thinkers believe that some measure of social justice should be used, and in this book I argue that social justice defined as fairness is the best one.

These beliefs of Progressive thinking give the state a key role in the economy, but it is important to understand that it is an enabling one, which is very different from the command-and-control role of traditional socialism or the minimalist role of neo-liberalism.

At the time of writing this book the prospects of the global economy are grim. Growth is slow or non-existent, incomes are stagnating, and for many poor and middle-class people declining, financial markets are unstable and governments are having to cut back on essential services. If we are to emerge from this disastrous situation I believe we will need to re-think some of the certainties of the macroeconomic theory which has dominated political debate for the last thirty-five years.

But this book is not concerned with macroeconomic policy, but with the supply-side policies that governments need to develop to achieve economic growth and social justice. In describing these policies I have focused on financial markets rather than labour markets. This is not because I believe there is no room for improvement of labour markets but because I believe that today financial markets are more of a problem than labour ones.

In the first half of the book I describe the failures of the neo-liberalism which has dominated political economy for the last thirty-five years, and develop a new Progressive political economy. In Chapter 1, I argue that a preliminary assessment of neo-liberalism shows that it has major flaws, and in Chapters 2 and 3, I look at why the economic growth rates of countries differ and what role the state should play in creating the best conditions for firms to innovate and grow. This enables me in Chapter 4 to set out a new Progressive political economy.

In the second half of the book I look at how this new Progressive political economy can be used to produce a programme of economic reform for a country. In Chapter 5, I describe the performance of some of the different varieties of capitalism we find in the world, and what lessons politicians and policy-makers should draw from attempts to change them. In Chapter 6, I look at how a programme of reform for the equity markets in the UK could be drawn up, and in Chapter 7, I look at recent changes to its national system of innovation and its education and training system, and what further reforms should be made to them. In Chapter 8, I show how the ideas of Progressive capitalism can be applied in developing countries, and in Chapter 9, I describe the role the Enabling State should play, and how it can be protected from sectional interests and its capability raised.

There will be some people who will try to portray this book as an attack on capitalism. But it should be seen as a defence of capitalism because a major theme of the book is that the failures of capitalism we have seen in recent years are not an inherent part of it, and can be curbed by a programme of economic reform.

I can think of few more challenging or socially valuable jobs than building up a high-value-added business in today's knowledge economy, and I have great admiration for the entrepreneurs and innovators who do so. The huge contribution they make to our society needs to be recognised and should be richly rewarded.

But their activities should not be confused with the

activities of those whose aim is to appropriate the wealth of others, whether by exploiting the lack of knowledge of investors, financial engineering and asset stripping, insider dealing or taking advantage of a monopoly. These activities make a negative contribution to the wealth of our society and lead to growing inequality, and the government should seek to bring them to an end.

A large number of books have been produced in the last couple of years describing the failures of neo-liberal capitalism which were revealed by the financial crash of 2008, and how a few of them could be corrected. It is once again possible to talk about the need for a growth strategy, and people have started to debate the desirability of an industrial policy, though no one today is any clearer about what this means than they were in the past.

But because none of these initiatives are informed by a clear view of the role of the state, and what it can and should do to enable the success of entrepreneurs, it is very unlikely that these initiatives will have much impact. I have, therefore, sought in this book to set out an alternative political economy to neo-liberalism, and to show how it can be used to develop policies which will help industry to innovate and grow. There was nothing inevitable about the financial crash of 2008, and the resulting economic misery, and we can reform our economic institutions so we live in a fairer and more prosperous society.

ONE

THE END OF NEO-LIBERALISM

With the bankruptcy of Lehman Brothers in 2008, the period of thirty-five years during which neo-liberalism had dominated political and economic thinking came to an end. As governments across the world sought frantically to save their financial systems it was no longer possible to argue that markets were self-regulating and that the state had only a minimal role to play in the economy.

As Joe Stiglitz has written:

September 15, 2008, the date that Lehman Brothers collapsed, may be to market fundamentalism (the notion that unfettered markets, all by themselves, can ensure economic prosperity and growth) what the fall of the Berlin Wall was to Communism. The problems with the ideology were known before that date, but afterward no one could really defend it.[1]

---

1   J. Stiglitz, *Freefall*, Penguin Books, 2010.

To describe the new Progressive capitalism that I believe should replace the neo-liberal one is the task of this book. But before we look at what this new version of capitalism should look like we need to be clear about what we mean when we talk about capitalism. In spite of the many books which have been written about the history of capitalism, about its past successes and failures, and about its different varieties, it is difficult to find a clear and simple definition which differentiates it from other economic systems.

I believe, however, that it can be defined for our purposes by two simple features. Firstly, economically it is a system in which most of the assets needed for production are privately owned and, secondly, it is a system where production is guided and income distributed largely through the operation of markets. It is these two features which differentiates the economy we have in most developed countries today from that of either, for example, feudal England or twentieth-century Russian Communism.

Two other points should be noted. Firstly, capitalism should be seen not just as an economic system but as a socio-economic system which people invented to enable them to produce and exchange goods efficiently, and which is made up of many institutions. These include most importantly the institutions which underpin markets, the institutions which govern the activities of firms, the institutions which affect the generation and transfer of technology (that is, an economy's national system of innovation) and a country's education and training institutions.

Secondly, capitalism is not a static system with a fixed set of rules and a permanent division of responsibilities between private enterprise and governments, but a system which has constantly been reinvented in response to economic crises and a changing economic environment. As Dani Rodrik has said:

> The last two centuries of economic history in today's rich countries can be interpreted as an ongoing process of learning how to render capitalism more productive by supplying the institutional ingredients of a self-sustaining market economy: meritocratic public bureaucracies, independent judiciaries, central banking, stabilising fiscal policy, antitrust and regulation, financial supervision, social insurance, political democracy.[2]

The Three Stages of Capitalism

In order to understand the intellectual challenge which producing a new political economy of capitalism involves, it is useful to look back at the three stages of capitalism which have spanned the last two hundred years.[3] The most important difference between these three stages of capitalism is the different theory held during each of them by politicians and policy-makers about the relationship between politics and economics, and between government and markets.

---

2   D. Rodrik, *One Economics – Many Recipes*, Princeton University Press, 2007.
3   A. Kaletsky, *Capitalism 4.0*, Bloomsbury, 2010.

The theory that people hold on the role of the state is very much influenced by their economic ideas. If they think that economies are essentially self-regulating and have few market failures then obviously they will argue that the state should have a very small role. If, on the other hand, they think economies are prone to instability and many market failures, they will give it a much larger role. And each of the three stages of capitalism was characterised by a very different set of economic ideas.

The first of these three stages ran roughly from the British victory over Napoleon in 1815 until the 1920s and the Great Depression in the United States. It was based on the ideas of Adam Smith, set out in 1776 in *The Wealth of the Nations*, and David Ricardo, and the marginalist revolution of Mill, Jevons and Walras in the 1870s. During this period politicians and policy-makers believed that in a capitalist system economics and politics should be treated as two almost unrelated spheres of human activity. While there was extensive and pragmatic action to ameliorate the harshest excesses of free markets, the idea that these excesses might be resolved by political reforms did not figure in economic thinking.

The only alternative to classical laissez-faire capitalism was Marxism, set out in Marx's *Das Kapital* in 1867, with its abolition of private property, money and people's competitive instinct. But the Marxists did not see a role for the state in managing economic activity and employment.

The second stage of capitalism started with the New Deal and was highly successful for forty years until it disintegrated in the stagflation of the 1970s. Capitalism was seen to have performed badly during the 1920s and to have failed miserably during the 1930s. It had also come to be seen as morally objectionable and to have been responsible for the Second World War. At the start of his book *Modern Capitalism*,[4] published in 1965, Andrew Shonfield wrote 'what was it that converted capitalism from the cataclysmic failure which it appeared to be in the 1930s into the great engine of prosperity of the postwar Western world?' And later on, referring to his generation, he stated 'it is hard for us to believe that the bleak and squalid system which we knew could, in so short a time, have adapted itself, without some covert process of total destruction and regeneration, to achieve so many desired objectives.'

A second factor which helped to create the new political climate was the increasing acceptance of Keynes's economic ideas as set out in his *General Theory* published in 1936. By demonstrating that the balance of supply and demand would not automatically ensure full employment and that the economy was unstable and subject to fluctuations, Keynes justified a new role for government. An active budgetary policy to reduce unemployment and business cycles was required, and no longer could everything be left to the market.

The three decades after the Second World War in Western Europe saw a significant increase in the part played by the state in economic affairs. It was also a period of remarkable

---

4   Andrew Shonfield, *Modern Capitalism*, Oxford University Press, 1965.

growth. Between 1950 and 1973 the GDP of Western Europe grew by 4.5 per cent per annum, more than twice as much per annum as it did over the whole of the nineteenth and twentieth centuries. By contrast the rate of growth of GDP in Western Europe for the period 1973 to 2000 was 2.1 per cent per annum, the same as for the annual rate over the last two centuries. The thirty years after the Second World War in Western Europe were truly a golden age for growth.

In the United States there was also a major increase in state intervention in the economy but it took place earlier, under the leadership of Franklin D. Roosevelt in the years preceding the Second World War. Under his leadership a large number of industry-regulating institutions and laws were established, including the Public Utility Holding Company Act, the Communications Act, the Social Security Act, the Civil Aeronautics Act, the Motor Courier Act, the Natural Gas Act, the Securities Exchange Commission and the Federal Housing Administration. There was also a vast expansion of government. Between 1920 and 1970 government employment grew almost fourteen times, with the majority of this being at the federal level; in many policy areas (urban policy and housing, transportation, employment and training, environmental protection, and others), the federal government became the key actor who set the rules, provided the money and made the decisions.

This belief in the central role of government was so strong that as late as 1974 the *New York Times* could write that

1975 'could usher in a fundamental transformation of the American economy towards increased government planning and controls'. Also, as in Europe, the period from 1947 to 1973 in America was a golden age for the economy: productivity grew on average 3 per cent per year. Real compensation (wages and benefits) per hour grew no slower than 13.7 per cent for each five-year period between 1950 and 1970, and unemployment during this whole period averaged less than 4.6 per cent.

The third stage of capitalism ran from roughly the middle of the 1970s until 2008. Towards the end of the 1960s output and productivity growth began to slow, and macroeconomic instability once again became a problem. Western countries responded with their normal remedies such as deepening the involvement of the government in the economy, but this strategy quickly encountered diminishing returns, and the 1970s saw a growing number of distributional conflicts and in time a collapse of the political consensus on the role of the welfare state, corporatist bargaining and Keynesian macroeconomic management.

This failure of economic policy led to a fundamental shift in the political climate, highlighted by the election of Mrs Thatcher as Prime Minister in the UK in 1979 and the election of Ronald Reagan as President of the United States in 1980. It also led in time to a worldwide upsurge in neo-liberal ideas. These were not a coherent and unified set of ideas but rather a political philosophy which believed that economic institutions should be allowed to evolve spontaneously, which was instinctively and strongly opposed to state interventions and in favour of markets, and which argued that freedom is the only value against which economic institutions should be judged.

It represented a partial return to the nineteenth-century laissez-faire tradition, and the prescriptions of neo-liberal economists for most economic problems were deregulation and privatisation. Instead of treating economics as a branch of politics, politics were now seen as a branch of economics. The state was no longer perceived as the all-knowing guardian of the public interest, and most economic ills were blamed on the past and present interventions of government. Markets should be used wherever possible to discipline and control politicians who were seen only to pursue their own interests.

As in the previous two stages, the neo-liberal stage of capitalism was heavily influenced by the latest economic thinking. In this case it was the economic ideas of Milton Friedman and his monetarist followers at the University of Chicago, whose ideas were closely related to the 'new classical' economic doctrines which once again argued that free competitive markets, undistorted by state intervention, would produce stability and full employment. In particular a number of theories, the Rational Expectations Hypothesis (REH), the Efficient Market Hypothesis (EMH) and the Policy Ineffectiveness Proposition, were used to buttress the case that markets do not need to be regulated and the government should not try to manage demand in the economy.

A Preliminary Evaluation of Neo-liberalism

The financial crisis of 2008 clearly raised very serious doubts about the economic theories underlying neo-liberalism. Also, after some thirty-five years in which it has been the dominant political economy in the world, the time has come to evaluate the impact of neo-liberalism in terms of economic growth, inequality and financial stability. No one who lived through the 1980s will doubt that neo-liberalism has provided some valuable insights into how a complex modern economy should be managed, but in comparison with the period 1945 to 1975 it has not performed well.

To make a final assessment of the impact of neo-liberalism is obviously an almost impossible task, and it is certainly not the aim of this book to do so. Nevertheless, it is possible to look at its impact from three angles which suggest that we need a new Progressive political economy to guide policy-makers in the years ahead.

In the first place, we can look at the impact of neo-liberalism on the world economy. As we have already seen, there was a sharp drop in the rate of growth of GDP in Western Europe and the United States in the period 1973 to 2000, when neo-liberal ideas were in the ascendancy, compared to the period 1950 to 1973, when state intervention was the preferred strategy. If we look at the world's per capita income we see that it grew by 3.1 per cent in the period 1960 to 1980, and by only 2 per cent in the period 1980 to 2000. Growth of per capita income in developing countries also decelerated from 3 per cent to 1.5 per cent between the two periods. As we shall also see later some of the most notable economic success stories of this period, countries like South Korea and Taiwan, had forms of capitalism far removed from the neo-liberal model.

None of these figures for growth conclusively prove that neo-liberalism has failed as a theory of political economy, but they certainly cast doubt on the idea that the financial instability and inequality produced by neo-liberalism can be justified by an increase in the rate of economic growth.

Secondly, we can look at the impact that neo-liberalism has had on inequality. This can be done most simply by looking at the United States, which is the country which has most obviously pursued neo-liberal policies.[5] The statistics are astonishing. Between 1979 and 2005 the top 0.1 per cent, that is, the top household out of every thousand households, received over 20 per cent of all after-tax income gains, compared with the 13.5 per cent enjoyed by the bottom 60 per cent of households. In other words the extra cash sum received by the roughly 300,000 people in the top 0.1 per cent was 50 per cent bigger than the extra cash sum received by the roughly 180 million in the bottom 60 per cent. Nothing like this had occurred in the forty years of shared prosperity that the US economy had enjoyed before the late 1970s, or in any other advanced industrial country.

It is also not the case that this incredible surge in the rewards going to the top 0.1 per cent led to an increase in

---

5   Jacob S. Hacker and Paul Pierson, *Winner-Take-All Politics*, Simon & Schuster, 2010.

economic growth in the United States. On average, between 1979 and 2006, economic growth per capita was essentially the same in the fifteen core nations of Europe as it was in the United States. The United States is, of course, richer but the gap between it and European countries has been stable since the 1970s.

The most common explanation of the capture of a rising share of the national income by the richest Americans is that it is due to 'skill-based technological change' but this is not an explanation that stands up to scrutiny. The people who hold this view argue that during the last thirty years or so there has been a massive shift towards more knowledge-based employment. Formal education and advanced skills have become much more valuable, and this has led to the growing divide between the highly educated and the rest of American workers.

The figures, however, do not support this explanation. A large amount of the inequality which has arisen since the 1970s has been due to 'within-group inequality', that is, inequality among people with the same education and skill levels, and this cannot be explained by reference to education because it is by definition among people with the same educational level or skills. If 'skill-based technological change' were the explanation, one would also expect to see its impact in other countries, but this is not the case. In terms of the top 1 per cent's share of national income the United States was not exceptional in the early 1970s. Germany, Switzerland, Canada and France – all had a higher share of national income going to the top 1 per cent a generation ago. But today in the United States, the top 1 per cent has the highest share (16 per cent) and the greatest increase (virtually a doubling) of advanced industrial countries.

What then is the cause of the vast increase of wealth at the top in the USA? The answer can be mainly found in two areas: executive pay and the growth of the financial sector. The first point to understand is that 40 per cent of those in the top 0.1 per cent are high-paid executives in firms outside the financial sector whose pay has risen by a staggering amount. In 1965, the average chief executive officer (CEO) of a large US corporation made around twenty-four times the earnings of the typical worker. By 2007, average CEO pay was accelerating towards three hundred times typical earnings, and in that year the average CEO of the 350 largest publicly traded companies made more than $12 million per year.

There are, of course, people who will argue that top executives earn more today because they are so much more valuable to companies than they once were. But here again the experience of other rich nations shows that the modern global economy does not inevitably increase salaries to the extent that they have risen in the United States. American CEOs are paid more than twice the average for other rich nations.

The pay of executives in America also takes a different form from that of executives in other countries. American CEOs, for example, receive much of their pay in short-term stock options which lack transparency and enable CEOs to make quick stock market gains through job cuts, restructuring or creative accounting. It is claimed that these schemes incentivise executives to focus on shareholder value but the manipulation of these schemes by some executives so as to provide themselves with the biggest gains suggests that what is involved here is 'board capture' rather than a focus on 'shareholder value'.

If we turn now to Wall Street and the growth of the financial sector, we find that nearly 20 per cent of the top 0.1 per cent are financial professionals. We also find that between 1975 and 2007 wages and salaries in the industry roughly doubled as a share of national earnings, and that between 1980 and 2007 financial service companies expanded their share of company profits from around 13 per cent to more than 27 per cent. The increase in wages and salaries is a similar story to the rise of executive pay but it is also the result of the introduction of a wide range of exotic new financial products. These made very little contribution to economic growth but enabled the financial sector to increase the number of transactions it handled, with financial institutions taking a cut of each one. They also enabled the financial institutions to increase their level of debt and the return to their shareholders, and to increase the complexity and opacity of their products in ways that advantaged insiders.

In the case of both the rise of executive pay and the growth of the financial sector, there are people who will argue that they represent the inexorable working of the market economy, but I believe that in both cases they represent major institutional failures. In the case of executive pay a failure of corporate governance, and in the case of the financial sector a failure to regulate it effectively.

The inequality generated in the USA by the rise of executive pay and the growth of the financial sector was in both cases made worse by the tax and welfare policies of the government. When one takes into account all federal taxes including income tax, payroll taxes, and corporate and estate taxes, tax rates on the rich have fallen dramatically. Those in the top 1 per cent pay rates that are a full third lower than they used to in 1970, despite the fact that they are much richer than those in the top 1 per cent were then.

The United States has also done less to resist rising inequality than the majority of rich countries. In these countries over the past few decades income redistribution has either held steady or actually risen. In America on the other hand between 1980 and 2003, for example, the percentage by which government taxes and benefits reduced inequality (as measured by the Gini Index, a common inequality standard) fell by more than a quarter.

The underlying story, however, of the last thirty-five years is the failure of the government to understand that its policies shape financial and labour markets, and that as a result it plays a major role in what has been called the 'pre-distribution' of income. Neo-liberals see the night-watchman state policing free markets, and not intervening in them, but this is an ideological position and not a description of reality.

Thirdly, as part of our preliminary evaluation of neo-liberalism, we can look at two situations where neo-liberal ideas were applied very aggressively: the collapse of the Russian economy in the 1990s and the deregulation which preceded the financial crash of 2008 in the USA. In both cases there was a major institutional and political failure, a decline in the economy and a vast transfer of wealth to a small, undeserving group of individuals.

The Collapse of the Russian Economy

In Russia, the collapse of Communism created an ideological vacuum that was quickly filled by numerous Western advisors who came to help put in place a market economy.[6] The main focus of their efforts, however, quickly became privatisation. The challenge they faced was a complex and difficult one but they believed that privatisation would solve all their problems.

There were three major problems they needed to tackle. Firstly, the industrial structures in Russia were not based on economic logic but on planned linkages within the regions of the ex-Soviet empire. They were isolated from world markets and they produced goods made better and more cheaply abroad. They were shielded from competition and exported on a large scale to similarly non-competitive markets. They also operated with constant output and input prices and had virtually unlimited access to credit. Few of them were capable of surviving in a competitive market environment.

Secondly, there was an absence of the institutions which are

---

6   J. Stiglitz, *Globalization and Its Discontents*, Penguin Books, 2002.

essential to the efficient functioning of capitalism. There were institutions which appeared to perform the same function as those in the West, but this was an illusion. There were institutions in Russia called banks, but they did not take in savings, make decisions about loans or ensure that loans were repaid. They simply allocated funds as they were instructed by the central planning agencies. There were companies in Russia, but they did not make entrepreneurial decisions. They simply produced what they were told to produce with the inputs they were given. The necessary legal, regulatory and social institutions did not exist to ensure that commercial contracts were enforced, that a minimum social safety net enabled restructuring to take place, that financial markets operated fairly or that competition was maintained.

Thirdly, there was a shortage of managers with entrepreneurial experience. The managers that the Communist system produced did not have the skills to operate in a market economy, and those with the best technical-managerial experience were to be found in the declining military-industrial complex. There was, however, a surplus of criminal experience.

Faced with this situation, there was a major debate between the school of reformers who wanted to move slowly, known as the gradualists, and the radical privatisers who wanted to move fast and who were described as being in favour of 'shock therapy'. The gradualists believed that the transition to a market economy would produce better results if the necessary institutions were put in place before privatisation took place, while the radical privatisers supported the idea of a rapid privatisation in order to quickly create a large group of people with a vested interest in capitalism.

The views of the radical privatisers were based on the neo-liberal theory that all one has to do to generate a functioning market economy is create private property. To be successful, all that privatisation has to do is transfer assets to the first private owners. They might not have the experience or skills to manage them, but the first private owners will only get the maximum price for their new assets if the active owners to whom they sell them know that their property rights will be secure. Therefore, the first owners will have every incentive to create and enforce the rules and regulations that protect private property.

The battle between the radical privatisers and the gradual-ists was won by the radical privatisers, and a rapid and massive programme of privatisation was launched. The results were disastrous. The assets of the Soviet state were transferred too rapidly to the private sector, with much former state property falling into the hands of criminals. Anatoly Chubais, the leader of the Russian economic reform process was revealingly reported as saying: 'They are stealing absolutely everything and it is impossible to stop them. But let them steal and take their property. They will then become owners and decent administrators of this property.'

But this did not happen. The new Russian oligarchs were more concerned to transform the assets they controlled into negotiable currency than to develop them, and having secured economic power they used it to extend their political power.

In 1997, a study which had been commissioned by the Central Bank and carried out by the Russian Academy of Sciences revealed that a small number of Russian oligarchs had amassed an estimated fortune of $140 billion. It also came to the conclusion that the oligarchs opposed both investing this money and developing a 'market acting according to law', because this would threaten their financial–political dominance.

The programme of privatisation led to the collapse of the Russian economy. The loss of GDP was greater than Russia suffered in the Second World War. In the period 1940 to 1946, industrial production in the Soviet Union fell by 24 per cent. In the period 1990 to 1999, it fell by almost 60 per cent. And as GDP declined, it was divided up more inequitably. While vast resources were concentrated in the hands of an astonishingly small proportion of the population, so that some of them grew truly rich by world standards, the majority of the population grew poorer. In 1989 only 2 per cent of those living in Russia were in poverty; by late 1998, that number had risen to 23.8 per cent, as measured by the $2 a day standard.

This appalling trajectory was not the result of accident or external events but of the choice of 'shock therapy' as the method of reform, and the reason it failed can be best summed up in the words of Stephen Cohen and Andrew Schwartz:

Creating a market-driven economy (and a political democracy) is not just about dismantling state regulations, controls, and capacity for action, distributing shares in giant monopolies, and running elections. It is, first, about building institutions. And the core of the Russian failure is in institution building, especially the key institution, a functioning state.[7]

The Financial Crash of 2008 in the USA

Turning now to the financial crash of 2008 in the USA, we see a different but equally disastrous institutional and political failure, much of which was mirrored in the UK, though on a less dramatic scale.[8] A key cause of the financial crash was the decision by Alan Greenspan and the Federal Reserve to keep the funds rate below 2.5 per cent from November 2001 to February 2005. The result was a borrowing binge by homeowners, consumers, businesses and speculators, and a massive housing bubble. It was, however, the twinning of this loose monetary stance with an explosive period of financial deregulation that proved to be disastrous for both the USA and the world economy.

As a result of the decision to keep the funds rate low between the end of 2002 and the end of 2006, the total amount of debt outstanding in the United States grew from $31.84 trillion to $45.32 trillion, an increase of $13.5 trillion or 42.3 per cent. This increase in debt amounted to about $43,000 for every

---

7   Stephen S. Cohen and Andrew Schwartz, 'Deeper into the Tunnel', in Stephen S. Cohen, Andrew Schwartz and John Zysman (eds), *The Tunnel At The End Of The Light*, University of Berkeley, 1998.

8   J. Stiglitz, *Freefall*, Penguin Books, 2010.
     J. Cassidy, *How Markets Fail*, Farrar, Straus and Giroux, New York, 2009.

person in the country, including children and senior citizens, or about $128,000 for each household.

The components of the $13.5 trillion increase are also important. While most attention has focused on the growth in mortgage debt, especially sub-prime loans, it should also be noted that over the same period, the indebtedness of the financial sector went from about $10.1 trillion to $14.3 trillion. Subsequently, it increased to $16 trillion by the end of 2007. This massive gearing of the financial sector was unprecedented in US history and made it very vulnerable to negative shocks.

The loose monetary stance pursued by Greenspan led predictably to a housing bubble, which equally predictably burst in mid-2007, and this in turn resulted in the economy going into recession in December 2007, Lehman Brothers going into bankruptcy in September 2008, and the American economy going into free fall in October 2008, raising the danger that it would take down much of the world economy with it. Such bubbles, and the disasters they bring, are as old as capitalism and banking itself, but what made it so lethal this time was that it followed an extensive period of deregulation and the growth of a number of so-called financial innovations which enabled the bubble to become bigger before it burst, increased its harmful impact when it did burst, and made it more difficult to untangle the mess afterwards.

During the years leading up to the financial crash of 2008, American financial markets did not perform the essential functions that society requires them to perform: mobilising savings, allocating capital and managing risk, while keeping transaction costs low. Instead, the absence of effective regulation allowed them to create risk, misallocate capital, and encourage excessive indebtedness while imposing high transaction costs. This they did by exploiting both customers and investors, with the result that the bloated financial markets were eventually able to capture 40 per cent of profits in the corporate sector.

Four major institutional failures contributed to the disastrous performance of the financial sector, all of which can be attributed to the lack of effective regulation. These were the uncontrolled growth of sub-prime mortgages and their securitisation; the high level of debt taken on by the banks; the lack of transparency of bank balance sheets and the use of 'special-purpose vehicles'; and the uncontrolled growth of derivatives. Each of these institutional failures had disastrous consequences, and in combination nearly proved fatal.

Almost certainly the greatest failure was the uncontrolled growth of sub-prime mortgages and their securitisation. Sub-prime mortgages are ones provided to borrowers who would normally not be regarded as creditworthy. Many of them were so-called 'Ninja' loans extended to people with no incomes, no jobs and no assets, and, therefore, with very little ability to repay them. The growth of these mortgages was very rapid in the early years of this century.

Sub-prime mortgages were below 10 per cent of all mortgage originations until 2004, but then grew to 20 per cent of the market at the peak in 2006. By March 2007 the value of US sub-prime mortgages was estimated at $1.5 trillion.

In view of the fairly remote possibility that these loans would ever be repaid, why did the market grow so fast? The answer is simple. Mortgage originators and banks found a way of providing mortgages to people, collecting their fees and then passing on the risks to others. This was done by securitisation, the packaging of large numbers of mortgages together and then selling on tranches of them, with different levels of risk, to investors.

The fatal flaw of this process was that it removed all incentive from the originating brokers to perform due diligence and monitor borrowers' creditworthiness, as most of the sub-prime loans they originated were subsequently securitised. As a result, when house prices began to fall at the end of 2006, the poor quality of the mortgages in mortgage-backed securities resulted in the value of the mortgage-backed securities falling very rapidly as default rates and repossessions escalated. The destruction of value for the financial institutions and investors probably approached $1 trillion.

The performance of the rating agencies also contributed to this massive institutional failure, and was the result of distorted incentives. Moody's and Standard & Poors were being paid by the banks that originated the securities they were asked to rate, and if one rating agency didn't give the grade that the investment bank wanted for the different tranches of a mortgage-based security, then the investment bank could turn to another.

The second major institutional flaw was the failure of the Securities and Exchange Commission to stop the banks taking on a high level of debt. By 2002, the big investment banks had a ratio of debt to equity – as high as twenty-nine to one. This means that a 3 per cent fall in asset values would bankrupt them, and the fact that the Securities and Exchange Commission allowed this to happen can only be explained by assuming that it had come to believe in the effectiveness of self-regulation: the idea that banks could be allowed to police themselves. As if this high level of leverage was not bad enough, the SEC, in a controversial decision in April 2004, seems to have given the banks more latitude, as some of them increased their leverage to forty to one. Here again, one can only assume that the regulators had been convinced that with better computer models, the banks were better able to manage risk.

The third major institutional flaw revealed by the financial crash was the way in which banks were able to move risk off their balance sheets and thereby prevent them from being properly assessed. Bear Stearns received an unqualified audit opinion on 28 January 2008, but by 14 March had to be taken over, with Federal Reserve assistance, by J. P. Morgan. The scale of deception can also be seen by the fact that Lehman Brothers could report that it had a net worth of some $26 billion shortly before its demise and yet have a hole in its balance sheet approaching $200 billion.

A major form of deception was the rise of special purpose vehicles (SPVs), also known as special investment vehicles (SIVs). These off-balance-sheet entities acted like mini banks. They issued short-term debt to investors and used the cash they raised to buy long-term assets from their parent companies such as mortgage securities, corporate loans and securitised car loans. Legally, these shell companies were independent entities, but to give investors reassurance about buying the short-term paper that the special purpose vehicles issued, their sponsor firms had provided them with guaranteed credit lines, which they could draw on as needed and which meant that in a financial crisis, all their debts came back onto their parent's balance sheet. The main purpose of these vehicles was to make the balance sheets of their parent companies look better, and the numbers were huge. The SIVs associated with Citigroup alone had assets of almost $100 billion. Markets can't work well without good information, and during this period the distorted balance sheets of banks did not enable market participants to interpret them in a meaningful way.

The fourth failure the financial crash revealed was the uncontrolled growth of derivatives. The value of derivatives, as one might expect from their name, is derived from some other asset. A bet that the price of stock will be greater than ten dollars in a week's time is a derivative. Derivatives can be used to manage risk, but the lack of regulation had disastrous consequences. Many institutions and investors had substantial positions in derivatives whose risk characteristics were poorly understood even by the most sophisticated of market participants. Furthermore, excessive risk-taking and poor counter-party risk management by many banks meant that the financial system was saddled with an enormous unrecognised level of systemic risk.

These four flaws of the financial markets, which were

revealed by the financial crash of 2008, were all due to poor regulation or a lack of regulation. Regulations serve many purposes. Two of the most important are stopping banks from exploiting poor or poorly educated people and ensuring the stability of the financial system. In the deregulatory frenzy of the 1980s, the 1990s and the early years of the last decade, US deregulators stripped away both kinds of regulations and paved the way for the financial crash. It is also clear that a key player in this process was Alan Greenspan, whose neo-liberal views can best be summed up in his own words: 'I do have an ideology. My judgement is that free, competitive markets are by far the unrivalled way to organise economies. We have tried regulations. None meaningfully worked.'

The financial crash of 2008 revealed some major institutional failures which resulted from an adherence to the neo-liberal model of capitalism that had been dominant for the last thirty-five years. But these flaws are not an inherent part of capitalism and it is not difficult to think of ways in which they could be rectified. For example, banks should be required to carry the activities of special purpose vehicles on their balance sheets, as they already are in Spain and Italy, and if they continue to be allowed to own hedge funds, these should be treated in the same way. What is required now is a major programme of economic reform so that a similar financial crash cannot happen in the future.

A Progressive Future

A preliminary evaluation of the neo-liberal theory of political economy in terms of economic growth, inequality and financial stability raises very serious doubts about its efficacy and, if there were no alternative to it, we would need to accept that our future and that of our children was one of low growth, rising inequality and frequent financial crises. But, as I will show, there is an alternative.

At the same time, Progressive politicians and policy-makers should not try to turn the clock back to some previous intellectual golden age. The command-and-control policies of traditional socialism were largely discredited in the 1960s and 1970s, which is why neo-liberalism came to be the dominant political economy in the Western world. No one wants to go back to a world of nationalisation, national plans and income policies. There are those who will argue that the flaws that have appeared in capitalism in recent years are an unavoidable part of it. But I believe that it is possible to develop a new Progressive form of capitalism which maintains the essential dynamism of capitalism but does not display the flaws that we have seen in recent years. In order to develop this new Progressive political economy we will in the next chapter take a closer look at why the economic growth rates of countries differ and what implications this has for the role for the state.

TWO

WHY ECONOMIC GROWTH RATES DIFFER

In the previous chapter we have seen that the dominant neo-liberal political economy of the last thirty-five years has not provided a useful policy framework for politicians and policy-makers. It has, overall, led to a reduction in the rate of growth, it has increased inequality and it has resulted in greater financial instability. A new Progressive political economy is therefore needed.

The central question of political economy is: what is the role of government in the economy? To answer this question we need to ask two further questions. The first: what are the conditions which lead to fast growth in a given country? The second: which of these is the state in the best position to provide? We need, therefore, a good understanding of the process of economic growth and why economic growth rates differ between countries.

In the long term, a nation's standard of living depends on the capacity of its firms to produce a higher and rising level of productivity in the industries in which they compete, and this in turn depends on their capacity to improve the quality of their products and services or achieve greater efficiency.[9] Productivity determines a nation's standard of living because it is the prime cause of national per capita income. The productivity of people determines their wages, while the productivity with which capital is employed determines the return it earns for those who have provided it. To achieve a high and rising level of productivity requires that a nation's firms must continually upgrade themselves by improving productivity in their existing industries. They must also develop the capabilities required to compete in more sophisticated industry segments and learn how to compete successfully in entirely new and more complex industries, as in both cases productivity is likely to be higher.

If there were no international competition, the level of productivity which a country's firms attained could be looked at separately from what was happening in other countries. International trade and foreign investment, however, both provide an opportunity to increase a nation's level of productivity and pose a danger that productivity will be reduced. International trade makes it possible for a nation to raise its productivity by eliminating the need for its own firms to produce all the goods and services that it wants. It can then specialise in those industries and segments where its firms have a productivity advantage, and import those products and

---

9   Michael E. Porter, *The Competitive Advantage of Nations*, Macmillan, 1990.

services where its firms are less productive than their foreign rivals; in this way it can raise the average productivity level of its economy.

On the other hand, if the more productive firms in a country lose out to foreign rivals, then the country's ability to sustain its productivity growth will be impacted negatively. And if firms transfer abroad highly productive activities because the environment enables them to be carried out there more profitably after taking account of foreign wages and other costs, that will also have a negative impact on the home country's level of productivity.

It should be understood that this dynamic view of economic growth is very different from the static view which is taken by much traditional economic thinking. In a static view of competition, a nation's factors of production are fixed, and firms shift them to where they will produce the greatest return. In a dynamic view of competition, however, innovation and change play an important role. Instead of firms simply shifting resources to where the returns are greatest, they seek to increase the returns available through new products and processes. Instead of deploying a fixed pool of factors of production, firms and nations seek to improve the quality of factors, raise the productivity with which they are utilised and create new ones.

If the ability of firms to increase their productivity by upgrading themselves in competition with foreign firms is seen to be the prime source of a country's rate of economic growth, then the accumulation of organisational and technological capabilities by firms must become a central concern of policy-makers. Neo-liberal economists have tended to focus solely on how well a nation's financial and labour markets allocate capital and labour, but this is clearly only a part of the explanation of why some countries grow faster than others. If we want to understand why some countries are more economically successful than others, we need to understand both how firms in some countries are able to accumulate organisational and technological capabilities faster than in others, thereby creating new and more productive opportunities for investment, and how financial and labour markets in those countries do a better job of allocating resources to those more productive activities.

I believe that there are three key factors which empirical studies have shown to be important in explaining the ability of firms to accumulate organisational and technological capabilities; three factors which tend to be ignored or misspecified in standard growth theory, including the new neo-classical growth models. These are: firstly, the governance and management of business firms. Secondly, technology as a body of understanding and practice, and the processes by which it is generated and used to create new products and production methods, and, thirdly, a country's education and training system, which is a key part of the environment within which firms operate.

The nature of firms themselves is very important in explaining their ability to accumulate organisational and technological capabilities. In the view of both old and 'new' growth theorists, the specifications of firms' governance and management are irrelevant. Firms can best be treated as black boxes and all that matters are the equilibria of production functions. But this is not the story business historians tell, whether they are discussing the role played by multi-divisional corporations in enabling the USA to forge ahead in the early part of the twentieth century, the contribution of firms to the growth of the German chemical industry, or the part played by the organisation of Japanese firms in their country's extraordinary growth performance in the post-World War II era.[10]

Economists have not shown much interest in the governance and management of firms because they mainly look at economies at the level of the whole economy or industrial sectors. It may also be the case that, at the level at which economists look at the economy, they believe that what firms do is determined by their environment, and that they regard firms as simply puppets dancing to the tune played by the market. I want to argue, however, that the way companies are governed and managed affects the rate at which an economy grows, and that Erik Reinert was right when he pointed out that by eliminating the differences between Microsoft and a twelve-year-old boy and his shoeshine 'firm' based in a Lima slum, economists also eliminate a potentially important reason why Bill Gates and his country are wealthier than the shoeshine boy and his country.[11]

---

10 James P. Womack, Daniel T. Jones and Daniel Roos, *The Machine that Changed the World*, Macmillan, 1990.

11 Erik S. Reinert, *How Rich Countries Got Rich — and Why Poor Countries Stay Poor*, Constable, 2007.

The second factor which is important in explaining the ability of firms to accumulate organisational and technological capabilities is technology. There are a number of ways of thinking about technology. One way is to see it as a set of blueprints which can be stored in a library and costlessly and instantaneously taken out and applied. But while it is true that much technology can be described in blueprints, texts, pictures and equations, it usually takes a highly trained professional to make sense of such blueprints. And access to such blueprints is usually only a first step to making a technology work. A great deal of learning by doing and using is required to gain a real mastery of it, and much of the knowledge involved is in the fingers as well as in the head.

As a consequence, such learning should not be seen as something which happens 'off line'. On the contrary, it takes place in companies and goes together with the acquisition of production equipment and the process of learning how to use that equipment and adapt it to local conditions. In turn, this goes hand-in-hand with the training of workers and engineers, and the formation of managers capable of efficiently running complex organisations.

If we want to understand fully how technological capabilities are accumulated, we need to make a distinction between firms at the technological frontier of their industry and those which are catching up. In the case of firms which are at the technological frontier of their industry, the accumulation of technological capabilities will involve inventive discovery and patenting. In the case of firms which are catching up, it will involve imitation, reverse engineering, adoption of capital-embodied innovations, learning by doing and learning by using.

The processes by which firms in a nation accumulate technological capabilities are complex, involve a number of different institutions and differ between countries. As a result they are known as national systems of innovation, and a great deal of research has gone into the effectiveness of different systems. They have been defined by Christopher Freeman as 'the network of institutions in the public and private sectors whose activities and interactions initiate, import, modify and diffuse new technologies',[12] and later in this chapter we will say more about how they work and what role the state needs to play in developing them.

The third factor which is important in explaining the ability of firms to accumulate organisational and technological capabilities is how well a country's education and training system performs its functions. This is not something that can be assessed simply by looking at the mean years of schooling in a country, though this is important. The relevance and quality of the education and training being given are also extremely important. An obvious feature of the successful growth of countries such as South Korea and Taiwan is the high proportion of engineers educated in their universities, and governments need to look carefully at whether, for example, there is a good technical stream in their schools.

---

12   Christopher Freeman, *Technology Policy and Economic Performance*, Pinter Publishers, 1987.

If we are to explain historical economic growth patterns, we need to understand how differences in the governance and management of a country's firms, national systems of innovation, and education and training systems affect its economic performance. Until recent years, these factors have not been given the prominence they should have in economists' explanations of growth patterns, a fact which has limited the usefulness of such explanations. As Richard Nelson has said, not including these variables is like trying to write a detective story without the detective, the murder and the murderer. And because, as we shall see in Chapter 4, all three factors involve institutions which need to be designed and reformed by government, their absence from explanations of economic growth gives a distorted view of the role of the government in the economy.

Two final points need to be made about the accumulation of organisational and technological capabilities by firms. Firstly, it is easy to conclude that with the globalisation of industries and the internationalisation of companies the nation has lost its role in the international success of firms. But the evidence strongly contradicts this idea. As we shall see again and again in this book, the leading firms in particular industries and segments of industries tend to be concentrated in a few nations and to sustain competitive advantage for many decades.

Competitive advantage appears to be created and sustained through a highly localised process which can be strongly influenced by government. Differences in national institutions and histories have an important influence on economic success, and the role of the home nation continues to be of great importance.

Secondly, in the preceding paragraphs I have argued that the accumulation of organisational and technological capabilities, largely but not exclusively in firms, is the fundamental driver of economic growth, but it should not be seen as a 'magic bullet'. It is essential that it is matched firstly by congruent macroeconomic policies and secondly by financial and labour markets which incentivise wealth creation rather than wealth appropriation. An economy needs to be allocatively efficient as well as providing the best possible conditions for the accumulation of organisational and technological capabilities.

The way that most of the institutions mentioned in this section function is, in general terms, well understood by most politicians and policy-makers. However, before looking at how differences in these institutions can be used to explain the different growth rates of countries, it is necessary to say something about how a country's national system of innovation works, as this is relatively a new term and not always well understood.

National Systems of Innovation

If we want to understand how national systems of innovation work we need first to analyse what we mean by this concept. There is, first of all, the use of the term 'innovation'. I think that Richard Nelson and Nathan Rosenberg[13] were right to

---

13 Richard R. Nelson and Nathan Rosenberg, 'Technical Innovation and National Systems', in Richard R. Nelson (ed.), *National Innovation Systems*, Oxford University Press, 1993.

interpret the term rather broadly to cover the processes by which firms master a new technology and turn it into products and manufacturing processes which are new to them, if not to everyone else in the world. The reason for taking this broad approach is that the differences between the activities and investments associated with being the first firm to bring a new product to the market or make use of a new manufacturing process, and those associated with staying at the leading edge of an industry, are not as great as people imagine. Also, if we are mainly concerned about economic performance, then it is certainly the broader concept of innovation which is most important rather than the determinants of being first.

Turning to the use of the word 'system', we mean simply that innovation in this context is driven forward by a number of elements and the relationship between them. There are those who prefer to talk about 'ecosystems' on the grounds that this makes it clear that they are something beyond the control of governments, but I can't see it makes any difference, and governments do obviously play a part in the construction of them.

There is, however, no implication that the set of institutions works smoothly and effectively together. The use of the term 'system' is simply used to make it clear that if we want to understand the innovative performance of a country we need to look at a number of elements and the relationship between them.

Finally, there is the concept of a 'national' system. To what extent is it correct to put most of the emphasis on national systems of innovation, as opposed to regional/local ones on one side and international ones on the other? There are, I think, two reasons for putting the most emphasis on national systems of innovation. The first is that most technological communities and networks that are the source of innovations operate on a national basis, though importantly there are some clusters of firms which operate on a regional or local basis and a few international technological communities. Secondly, the vast majority of policy decisions and institutional design decisions made by government that affect the innovation performance of firms are taken on a national basis. So if we are interested in improving them, we need to think in national terms.

Having clarified what we mean by national systems of innovation we now need to focus on the actors who populate them. At their centre, of course, are firms, as most innovations are developed by firms. The introduction of the in-house industrial research laboratory in the nineteenth century was one of the most important developments in the history of national systems of innovation, and many studies show that the interactions between different departments within firms (such as marketing, production and R&D), as well as the involvement of the workforce, are of critical importance in a country's innovation performance. The Japanese, for example, have excelled at incremental innovation partly because of the horizontal flow of information in Japanese companies, as opposed to the vertical flow characteristic of the large hierarchical American corporation.

The role of the modern research university in national systems of innovation is also very important, both as a place where industrial scientists and engineers are trained and also as the source of research findings and technical developments of relevance to new products and processes in industry. Throughout much of the nineteenth century it was not necessary for an inventor to have a strong formal education in science, though from time to time inventors would consult scientists, but by 1910 or so, the time when an unschooled genius such as Thomas Alva Edison could make major advances in electrical technologies was coming to an end. And in the twentieth century, firms have increasingly drawn on the research of universities in order to make radical breakthroughs. Intermediate technology bodies, intellectual property laws and standards organisations also play a role in the process of innovation, and government as a major user of innovations developed in the private sector can also have a beneficial impact on the demand for innovation.

For policy-makers and politicians trying to understand how national systems of innovation work, and how, therefore, they can be improved, two features need to be highlighted: the complex interaction between the supply side and the demand side, and the important role played by clusters. As Christopher Freeman has pointed out, in the 1960s and 1970s it was claimed that innovation was mainly a demand- or market-led activity, that most ideas which led to innovation did not come from R&D but from other parts of the firm or firm users, and that research was, therefore, a waste of resources for the firm since it could not lead to profitable innovations.[14]

However, a careful analysis of the surveys which have been cited to support these propositions does not do so, and instead shows a complex interaction between the 'supply' side (R&D labs and scientific and technical institutions) and the 'demand' side (potential and actual users, marketing organisations etc.). The explanation of this complex interaction lies, I believe, in the difference between incremental innovation and radical innovation.

Where incremental innovation is concerned, the experience of users is likely to be important and will often be the main source of ideas for improvement. But in the early stages of radical innovations, the contributions of scientific and technical institutions are likely to be most important and will often be the main source of ideas for improvement. This is not surprising, because radical innovations, such as synthetic dyestuffs or electric motors, are by definition ones that could not emerge from incremental improvement of existing products by users and therefore require a different source of ideas.

The second feature of national systems of innovation that policy-makers and politicians need to understand is the important role played by clusters of innovative firms. Michael Porter has described them as 'geographic concentrations of interconnected companies, specialised suppliers, service

---

14   Christopher Freeman 'Formal Scientific and Technical Institutions in the National System of Innovation', in Bengt-Ake Lundvall (ed.), *National Systems of Innovation*, Anthem Press, 2010.

providers, firms in related industries, and associated institutions (for example, universities, standards agencies, and trade associations) in particular fields that compete but also co-operate'.[15] They are important because they enable firms in the cluster to gain competitive advantage.

The most famous historical examples of clusters are the cotton textiles industry starting in Lancashire in the 1780s, the first iron steamships localised in and around Glasgow from the 1820s, the birth of electrical engineering in Berlin in the 1870s, and the start of automobile manufacturing in Detroit around 1900. Recent examples of clusters include the growth of electronics in Silicon Valley in the 1950s and in the suburbs of Tokyo in the 1980s, and the growth of the Cambridge cluster in England at the end of the twentieth century. It is important to realise, however, that clusters are not limited to 'high-technology' industries but extend to such areas as carpets around Dalton, Georgia in the USA, financial services in the City of London, the wine industry in California and the Italian footwear and fashion cluster.

Why do clusters exist and why are they so important to a country's innovative performance? If we analyse them in depth, the answers to these two questions can be found in the linkages, complementarities and spillovers of technology, skills, information, marketing and customer needs that are the basis of competitive advantage and are essential for innovation and the growth of firm productivity. It was these features of

---

15   Michael E. Porter, *On Competition*, Harvard Business School Press, 1998.

clusters that Alfred Marshall recognised when he wrote about industrial districts in his *Principles of Economics*:[16]

> When an industry has chosen a locality for itself, it is likely to stay there long: so great are the advantages which people following the same skilled trade get from near neighbourhood to one another. The mysteries of trade become no mysteries; but are as it were in the air, and children learn many of them unconsciously. Good work is rightly appreciated, inventions and improvements in machinery, in processes and the general organisation of the business have their merits promptly discussed: if one man starts a new idea, it is taken up by others and combined with suggestions of their own; and thus it becomes the source of further new ideas.

A number of lessons for policy-makers and politicians can be drawn from the history of successful clusters which illustrate three of the major themes of this book. The first is that today, the most important sources of competitive advantage are created and not inherited. Inherited competitive advantage such as natural resources, geographic location or a supply of labour is becoming less important. Prosperity increasingly depends not on inherited inputs, but on creating the conditions that allow firms operating in a region to be highly productive in the use of inputs. Secondly, the presence of clusters suggests that part of what makes a company highly competitive lies

---

16   Alfred Marshall, *Principles of Economics*, Macmillan, 1920.

outside the company, residing in the location of its business units. As Michael Porter has written, 'The odds of building a world-class mutual fund company are much higher in Boston than in most any other location; a similar statement applies to textile-related companies in North and South Carolina, high-performance auto companies in southern Germany, or fashion shoe companies in Italy'. Thirdly, in advanced regions, prosperity relies heavily on the ability of firms to innovate. If a firm does not innovate it will be caught up by firms in developing countries and regions that are continuously improving their skills and can easily access modern technology. Advanced regions, therefore, have constantly to upgrade their industries, or other countries will catch them up.

The above description of the way that national systems of innovation work makes it very clear, I think, why they are so important for the study of economic growth. The fact that neo-liberal economists have paid so little attention to them might suggest that the concept is a very new one. But they go back at least to the nineteenth century and the German economist, Friedrich List, author of *The National System of Political Economy* (1841). Christopher Freeman has rightly said the book could just as well have been called *The National System of Innovation*.

List was mainly concerned with how underdeveloped countries, as Germany then was, could catch up with England, and he advocated not only the protection of infant industries but also a broad range of policies to accelerate learning about new technology and its application. A single quotation from his book indicates the extent to which he anticipated many contemporary theories of 'National Systems of Innovation'. He wrote:

> The present state of the nations is the result of the accumulation of all discoveries, inventions, improvements, perfections and exertions of all generations which have lived before us: they form the mental capital of the present human race, and every separate nation is productive only in the proportion in which it has known how to appropriate those attainments of former generations, and to increase them by its own acquirements.[17]

He also argued strongly that industry should be linked to the formal institutions of science and education:

> There scarcely exists a manufacturing business which has no relation to physics, mechanics, chemistry, mathematics or to the art of design etc. No progress, no new discoveries and inventions can be made in these sciences by which a hundred industries and processes could not be improved or altered. In the manufacturing State, therefore, sciences and arts must necessarily become popular.[18]

Having sought to describe what is meant by a national system

---

17 Friedrich List (1841), *The National System of Political Economy*, Dent, London (English edn 1909).
18 Ibid.

of innovation and how such systems work, we now need to see whether this concept, together with changes in other institutions, can be used to explain the different economic growth rates of different countries. For this purpose I have chosen two case studies of unexpected economic success: the rapid economic growth of Japan between 1955 and 1973 followed by a period of much diminished growth, and the growth of the Finnish economy in the 1990s. These case studies look at different countries at very different times, but in both cases there was a sharp change in economic performance.

The Rapid Economic Growth of Japan between 1955 and 1973

The rapid growth of Japan between 1955 and 1973, the year of the worldwide oil shock, and its diminished rate of growth during the period 1975 to 1990, is an important and interesting success story against which to test the idea that national systems of innovation and other institutional changes have a major impact on economic growth. From 1955 to 1973, Japan's GDP per worker leapt from $3,500 to $13,500. Japan also achieved an annual growth rate of 8.4 per cent in this period, which was far higher than any other country, including the Newly Industrialising Countries (NICs), achieved during the same stage of development. But during the period 1975 to 1990, when GDP per worker went from $13,500 to $22,500, its annual growth was only 3.5 per cent, which was below what some other countries achieved at a similar stage.

The reason for its differential performance between these two periods can, I think, be attributed to its institutions and, in particular, its national system of innovation. There were four factors which had a very beneficial impact on Japan's economic performance as it sought to catch up with Western Europe. These were: the role of the Ministry of International Trade and Industry (MITI); the role of companies' research and development strategies in relation to imported technology and 'reverse engineering'; the role of education and training and related social innovations; and the conglomerate structure of industry.

Japanese firms rapidly accumulated organisational and technological capabilities between 1955 and 1973, and their success was greatly aided by social and institutional changes promoted, and sometimes initiated, by MITI. In the immediate post-war period, Japan, after an intense debate, rejected a long-term development strategy based on the traditional theory of comparative advantage, which was being advocated at that time by the Bank of Japan. It decided not to pursue a strategy based on its relatively low labour costs and comparative advantage in labour-intensive industries such as textiles, and instead sought a solution to its economic difficulties by upgrading its organisational and technological capabilities.

MITI thought in dynamic terms, and saw one of its key functions as being the promotion of the most advanced technologies with the greatest world market potential in the long term. The government, therefore, provided subsidies for the experimental installation and trial operation of new machines and equipment, tax support for research and development, and protection for infant industries, as well as helping companies to achieve inter-industry synergies. It also developed regional policies to strengthen technological capability throughout the country, particularly in small and medium-sized firms, by setting up nearly 200 Prefecture laboratories to offer research and technical advisory services.

A second factor which greatly affected Japan's economic success, and which went back to before the Second World War, was a strategy of importing and whenever possible improving the best available technology in the world. The method of assimilating and improving imported technology was mainly a form of reverse engineering. Instead of seeking to attract foreign direct investment, or the acquisition of blueprints for product and process design, Japanese companies attempted to manufacture a product similar to one available on the world market.

As a result, Japanese management, engineers and workers became accustomed to thinking of the entire production process as a system, and to thinking in an integrated way about product design and process design. This capability to redesign an entire production system became one of the major sources of Japanese success in industries as diverse as ship building, motor vehicles and colour televisions. In contrast, in many Third World countries, technology transfer took place either through subsidiaries of multinationals or the import of turn-key plants designed and constructed by foreign contractors. Neither of these methods was likely to lead to as valuable an accumulation of organisational and technological capabilities in the passive recipient enterprise.

A third factor which contributed greatly to Japan's economic success was a huge increase in the scale of education and training in Japan after the Second World War. Japan moved ahead of both West Germany and Great Britain in terms of the absolute numbers of young people acquiring higher levels of education, especially in science and engineering, and also in the scale and quality of industrial training carried out mainly or entirely at enterprise level.

Japan overtook the United States in the number of graduating electronic engineers early in the 1970s, and in 1977 on a per capita basis Japan had almost three times as many electronic and electrical engineers as the United States and four times as many as the United Kingdom. These improvements in education and training were also combined with social innovations such as quality circles and the abolition of the distinctions between blue and white-collar workers, which provided a good basis for continuous improvement through workforce involvement in technical change.

The fourth factor which contributed greatly to Japan's economic success was the important role played by the *keiretsu*, the large groups or conglomerates which succeeded the pre-War *zaibatsu*. These were particularly important in post-war Japan because they enabled Japanese firms to exploit the advantages of scale in technology, and in access to capital and markets, before they had individually become very large. In the rapidly expanding post-war economy they also enabled many new firms to enter the fastest-growing industrial sectors.

Having looked at the four key factors which contributed greatly to Japan's economic success, we now need to return to the question of why Japan in the period between 1955 and 1973 performed better than other countries at a similar stage of development, and worse in the period 1975 to 1990. The answer, I think, is an institutional one. In the 1950s and 1960s, Japan's institutions were ones appropriate for a 'development state' and they worked very effectively because Japan had a range of infant industries which needed help to become internationally competitive, and because it was at a stage of development when inter-industry synergies were very important.

Japan in the 1950s and 1960s had a range of industries, from autos to electronics, which had the potential to become world-class competitors, but they had not acquired either the economies of scale or the learning-by-doing efficiencies necessary to be internationally competitive and they therefore needed the protection and promotion of government if they were not to be strangled at birth.

A classic example is cars. Japan had some experience of car production before the Second World War, but after the war the industry was not in a position to stand on its own feet.[19] For example, during a brief period of liberalised trade in 1953, when Japan was producing only 5,000 cars a year, some 30,000 inexpensive European cars flooded in, overwhelming

---

19   Richard Katz, *Japan – The System That Soured*, M. E. Sharpe, 1998.

domestic output, and it looked for a time as if the car industry would be wiped out.

Because there are still neo-liberal economists who argue that the Japanese government's policies had no beneficial impact, it is worth looking in detail at what action the government took, and how it helped to produce a world-beating industry.

As we have already noted, there was a debate between 1949 and 1951 involving MITI and the Bank of Japan about the development strategy Japan should pursue. The Bank of Japan and the economists of the World Bank argued that the auto industry was too capital-intensive for a country such as Japan, which was short of capital. With its supply of cheap labour, Japan should instead concentrate on labour-intensive items like toys and textiles, and import the cars it needed.

But MITI went ahead and largely stopped the import of cars. At that time, under the 1949 Foreign Exchange Law, anyone who needed foreign exchange for any import had to get it from MITI and MITI simply refused to provide foreign exchange for the import of foreign cars beyond a minimal quota. In 1965, when the industry had become internationally competitive and almost 10 per cent of its output was being exported, the quota system was abandoned, but it was promptly replaced by a prohibitively high tariff rate of 40 per cent.

Besides import protection, the government also gave the industry large subsidies to help it fund the huge investments it needed in order to become internationally competitive. These included not only huge tax breaks and low-interest loans to the car-makers themselves, but also significant help to their key supplier industries such as auto parts, machine tools and steel.

As a result of this aid, the auto industry became one of the great Japanese economic success stories. By 1985 it had become the world's largest auto industry. It exported 54 per cent of its output, accounted for 26 per cent of all Japanese exports and 11 per cent of all manufacturing output, and developed new techniques for manufacturing cars, such as Toyota's famed just-in-time manufacturing system, which revolutionised the way cars were made across the world.

The second reason government support for industry in Japan was so effective is that Japan at this time was at a stage of development when inter-industry synergy was very important. The car industry, for example, was also one of the largest customers for the priority industries such as steel, machinery and electronics. If the car industry grew then this increased the demand for steel, which in due course lowered the cost of steel, which in turn lowered the cost of cars and led to greater demand for them. Similar economies of scale and inter-industry synergies applied to TVs and semiconductors.

The success of the policies of the Japanese government at this stage of its economic development has been well summarised by Michael Porter in his book *The Competitive Advantage of Nations*.[20] In it, having described what he called the 'relatively heavy-handed' role of the Japanese government after the Second World War, Porter wrote:

---

20   Michael E. Porter, *The Competitive Advantage of Nations*, MacMillan, 1990.

In the early Japanese successes, such as steel, shipbuilding and sewing machines, this sort of government role was constructive. Price was important to competitive position in the segments in which Japanese firms competed. Many of the industries were capital-intensive. Competitive advantage depended on having modern, large-scale facilities. Government's levers at this stage were powerful ones. Important Japanese industries were able to move beyond reliance on basic factor costs.

But if Japan's 'development state' institutions were able to outperform other countries in the period 1955 to 1973, why did it do worse in the period 1975 to 1990? The answer is that the institutions which did so well in the era of Japan's industrial takeoff were dysfunctional once Japan's economy had matured. But Japan did not abandon them, and what had been a strength became a weakness.

The most obvious feature of an economy at the start of its period of industrial takeoff is the presence of many infant industries. But by the 1970s, when Japan had matured economically, there were no more infant industries needing a helping hand in order to become internationally competitive. In the late 1950s Japan's economy had so many industries that exhibited economies of scale that on average, a 100 per cent increase in inputs yielded a 140 per cent increase in output. As Japanese industry matured, the returns to scale steadily came down, so that by the late 1970s Japan no longer enjoyed advantageous economies of scale.

But instead of modifying its 'development state' institutions at this point, Japan continued with them, though largely in a different form. As a result of joining GATT (the General Agreement on Tariff and Trade) in 1955, Japan had to eliminate quotas in order to adhere to GATT's free trade rules. Japan dragged out the process and then replaced the quotas with large tariffs. As late as 1978, the effective rate of tariff protection for manufacturing was 22 per cent. And MITI and MOF (Ministry of Finance) actively strengthened *keiretsu* ties and industry collusion in order to protect Japanese industry. This strategy was a serious mistake. Once a country's economy has matured and innovation rather than investment is the source of competitive advantage, the role of government has to change. As Michael Porter has written: 'Allocation of capital, protection, licensing controls, export subsidy and other forms of direct intervention lose relevance or effectiveness in innovation-based competition.'[21]

This failure to adapt the country's institutions to its changing economic circumstances was at least partly due to its failure to create a European-style welfare state. The system of lifetime employment worked reasonably well at a time when industry was growing fast, but it could not cope with a situation which involved a major restructuring of industry.

As Japan's economy began to slow in the 1970s and the government came under political pressure from progressives, it had the opportunity of creating a European-style welfare state. But

---

21   Michael Porter, ibid.

the government consciously decided not to do so. The conservative LDP was ideologically opposed to creating a Japanese
welfare state, fearing it would weaken work incentives, and the
Ministry of Finance was determined to restrain public spending.
While Prime Minister Tanaka declared that 1973 was the 'First
Year of the Welfare Era', the Ministry of Finance used the erod-
ing fiscal situation to slow the growth of welfare spending.

As a result, without a way of compensating the losers who
bear the costs of restructuring, the Japanese government was
forced to follow what has been called an 'employment pres-
ervation route'.[22] It increased spending on public works, and
the institutions of its 'development state' came increasingly
to be used for political aims. The Fiscal Investment and Loan
Program, which had helped channel funds from the National
Postal Savings System, public pensions and other sources to
development projects in the post-war period was redirected
towards political ends, and MITI focused its efforts on managing
declining industries rather than promoting growth industries.
Japan became, in the words of Richard Katz, 'a great nation
trapped in the straitjacket of obsolete institutions'.[23]

The Growth of the Finnish Economy in the 1990s
Turning now to the Finnish economy, up until the 1990s the
Finnish economy was not seen as a dynamic one, being largely

---

22 Jonah D. Levy, Mari Miura, and Gene Pack, 'Exiting Etatisme? New Directions
    in State Policy in France and Japan' in Jonah D. Levy (ed.), *The State After Statism*,
    Harvard University Press, 2006.
23 Richard Katz, *Japan: The System That Soured*, M. E. Sharpe, 1998.

dependent on the country's natural resource endowment. Its three largest industrial clusters were pulp and paper, wood products and engineered metal products. In 1970, pulp and paper accounted for 40 per cent of exports, wood products for 16 per cent, and engineered metal, including shipbuilding, for 23 per cent. By 2001, however, Finland had become one of the fastest-growing and most competitive economies in the world, and in the competitiveness rankings of the Global Competitiveness Report, Finland took top spot from the United States in 2000.[24]

That such a transformation would take place must have looked very unlikely in the early 1990s; the decade began with the most severe crisis the Finnish economy had ever experienced. In 1991 real GDP fell by 6.2 per cent and in 1992 it lost another 3.3 per cent. Exports dropped by 13 per cent in dollar terms in 1991 and unemployment rose from 3.5 per cent in 1990 to 17.9 per cent in 1993.

The reasons for this crisis are not difficult to find. The Berlin Wall had come down in 1989 and the economy of the Soviet Union, on which the Finnish economy was highly dependent, was collapsing. In addition, in the late 1980s the Finnish economy had taken on a huge increase in credit due to its liberalised banking sector, with the result that property prices and inflation rose, the Finnish exchange rate came

---

24 Örjan Sölvell and Michael E. Porter, *Finland and Nokia: Creating the World's most Competitive Economy,* Harvard Business School Case, 2011. Manuel Castells and Pekka Himanen, *The Information Society and the Welfare State — The Finnish Model,* Oxford University Press, 2002.

under pressure, and in September 1992 Finland was forced to float its currency and adopt tough macroeconomic policies.

Finland's economy began to grow again in 1993, with real GDP growth reaching 4 per cent, and staying at between 3.8 per cent and 6.3 per cent throughout the rest of the 1990s. In the period 1992–2002, labour productivity in the Finnish business sector grew by an annual average of 3.5 per cent and in the manufacturing sector the growth was 7 per cent, led by the telecommunications sector, which increased its productivity by an annual 25 per cent. The transformation of Finnish industry could also be seen in the changing composition of its exports. In 1999, pulp and paper accounted for 30 per cent of exports, as did electronics, while engineered metal products accounted for another 20 per cent.

This growth was fuelled to a large extent by the Finnish economy's strong performance as a producer of information technology. The IT sector became the most dynamic and competitive export sector. While in 2000 the cluster only employed 3 to 4 per cent of the labour force, it accounted for one-third of total exports and about 45 per cent of the Finnish GDP. At the core of this IT cluster was Nokia, the company which gave it a special strength in wireless telecommunications as well as its name of 'mobile valley'. Having started life as a wood-pulp paper mill in 1865 in the town of Nokia, by the late 1980s it had become a conglomerate with eleven divisions producing everything from toilet paper, rubber boots and car tyres to cables, computers and televisions. However, faced with a financial crisis in 1992 it divested itself of all of its businesses outside of telecommunications, and during the 1990s became the world leader in digital phones with a market share of 31 per cent in 2000. In that year its sales were €30.4 billion, with an operating profit of €5.8 billion, generating an above-profit margin for the industry. The company employed 60,000 people, 24,000 of whom were located in Finland, and had production locations in ten countries, R&D in fifteen countries and sales in over 130 countries.

There is, however, more to Finland's IT sector than Nokia. Nokia has some 300 suppliers in Finland but the entire Finnish IT cluster includes more than 3,000 companies, and Nokia's suppliers are not only working for Nokia. Finland, not just Nokia, has become a node in the global network of innovation, so that in the event of a catastrophic failure by Nokia, similar to the one that nearly happened at the beginning of the 1990s, parts of Nokia would likely be taken up by new or existing companies, in the same way as Nokia itself has collected parts of Finnish IT expertise throughout its history. A failure by Nokia would, however, certainly lead to a loss of economic growth and require an extremely difficult period of adaptation.

The Finnish success story can largely be attributed to its national system of innovation, which was to some extent consciously designed, the term itself having been introduced into Finland in 1990 by the Science and Technology Council. The national system of innovation can be best described by looking at how the main elements of it were gradually assembled. In reaction to a growing perception that Finland's economy was losing ground internationally, throughout the 1980s a series of new policies were brought in to stimulate innovation. In 1982 the government made a decision-in-principle to raise national research and development investment from 1.2 per cent of GDP to 2.2 per cent by 1992. Then in 1983, reflecting the perceived need for a conscious national technology policy, the National Technology Agency, Tekes, was founded to finance technology research and development as an independent agency reporting to the Ministry of Trade and Industry. This in turn led in 1986 to the National Science Policy Council, which had been founded in 1963, being transformed into the Science and Technology Policy Council.

Viewed from an international perspective, this body is exceptional for two reasons. Firstly, science and technology are treated together in the same council. Secondly, the importance attached to the Council is exemplified by the fact that its meetings are chaired by the Prime Minister and its membership includes eight key ministers (the Ministers of Education and of Trade and Industry are the vice-chairmen), ten of the highest-level representatives of Finnish Universities (rectors and top researchers), industry, the Finnish Academy, Tekes and employers' and employees' organisations. As a result, the shared vision that the Council develops spreads to the key participating bodies from the top down.

Finland met its 1982 research and development investment goal in 1992 and set new, higher goals. In 1996, still partly suffering from the recent recession, the Finnish government nevertheless decided to further increase research and development investment to 2.9 per cent of GDP by 1999, although at the time it was cutting public expenditure. This new goal was reached in 1998 and currently the share is estimated to be 3.2 per cent, making Finland, with Sweden, world leaders in research and development as measured by its share of GDP.

The Finnish Academy is focused on funding basic scientific research, while Tekes has become the main channel for business-oriented public research and development finance. According to international evaluations, Tekes has been very efficient in funding research and development that aims at exportable products. From an international perspective, Tekes' strength is its strong independent status. In many other countries similar activities are organised by the parliament or the relevant ministry, but Tekes has significant autonomy. Although Tekes is responsible to the Ministry of Trade and Industry, it takes decisions on funding itself. Tekes acts both proactively and reactively, and networking in its programmes among companies and between companies and universities is well rewarded.

The funding of Tekes for the very specific goal of advancing technology research and development work has also had a positive impact by clarifying the role of Sitra, the Finnish National Fund for Research and Development, which was founded in 1967 with considerable freedom to pursue its objectives both through direct financing of companies and through its own creative projects. Since Tekes was founded, Sitra has not funded technology research and development as such, but has evolved into a venture capitalist that finances the beginnings and expansion phases of start-up companies.

In 1990, the Science and Technology Policy Council conducted a major review of Finland's economic position that resulted in two further reform initiatives. The first, the Centre of Expertise Programme, focused on strengthening regional competitiveness by increasing innovation, renewing the regional production structure and creating new jobs in selected expertise areas. The second, the Cluster Programme, focused on developing the innovative capacity of industrial clusters by supporting cluster-specific R&D efforts. In parallel, the government set up fifteen incubators in proximity to regional clusters throughout Finland to make venture capital available for start-up companies.

The cluster approach was introduced in Finland in a study co-ordinated by the Research Institute of the Finnish Economy (ETLA) in the early 1990s, and outlined in 1993 in the White Paper 'A National Industrial Strategy' by the Ministry of Trade and Industry. The central message for policy-makers was that all government actions had implications for national competitiveness. Therefore, economic and industrial policies needed to be considered from an extensive perspective beyond the administrative boundaries of sectoral ministries. The cluster model stimulated new forms of interaction and co-ordination between ministries, public and private research units, and companies. The study further clarified the policy direction which had first started in the 1980s, in which the role of government was to create favourable framework conditions and which emphasised inter-organisational co-operation as well as the accumulation and transfer of know-how.

Four final points need to be made about Finland's economic success. Firstly, the Finnish national system of innovation is not just a list of factors but also a valuable network of interactions. For example, according to the Second European Community Innovation Survey, 53 per cent of Finnish innovative companies had co-operation agreements with universities in 1994 to 1996, compared with an EU average of 7.5 per cent.

Secondly, the state has played, and continues to play, a major role in guiding economic growth and building the information society in Finland. But it has not brought the economy under bureaucratic control. Instead it has been a major liberaliser of the economic system: for example, its effort to deregulate and globalise the Finnish telecommunications sector earlier than most other European countries was a decisive contribution to the new model of economic growth. The Finnish state has used incentives and strategic planning to implement market mechanisms, rather than substituting itself for them.

Thirdly, a basic building block of its economy is a totally free, high-quality public education system from kindergarten to the university, with one of the highest combined educational enrolment rates and a strong emphasis on engineering.

Finally, it should be noted that Finland's economic success took place at a time when it had a fully-fledged welfare state, and that such a welfare state seems to be compatible with technological innovation and a competitive market. In fact it may be essential for innovation and competition because the protection it provides makes workers less fearful of redundancy, and as a result increases work flexibility in a dynamic economy.

Lessons for Policy-Makers

A number of lessons for policy-makers should be taken away from the review in this chapter of the economic success stories of Japan and Finland. Firstly, if we want to understand why economic growth rates differ among countries, we need to look not only at how well their different market systems for allocating labour and capital work but also at the institutions they have for accumulating organisational and technological capabilities.

Secondly, while it is not possible to provide quantitative information to prove the point, the evidence seems to show that national systems of innovation have a significant impact on the ability of firms in a country to accumulate organisational and technological capabilities, and that governments can use the concept of national systems of innovation to create the right conditions for firms to innovate and grow.

Thirdly, well-designed institutions for social protection, such as unemployment pay, should not be seen as a hindrance to a dynamic economy and economic growth, but rather as a key factor in providing the work flexibility necessary for economic success.

Having looked in this chapter at why countries' rates of economic growth differ, in the next chapter we will look at what developed countries need to do to meet the challenges of the global economy, and how they can stay ahead of China as it races to the top.

THREE

THE RACE TO THE TOP

Globalisation

If we want to appreciate the challenges facing industry, it is necessary to understand not only the sources of economic growth, but also the impact that globalisation is having. The term 'globalisation' is used very loosely today to describe many changes in our economy and society. It is therefore important to focus on the central idea, which is that changes in the international economy are leading to the emergence of a single world market for labour, capital goods and services. This change has been brought about by a number of political, economic and technological changes that have exposed the nations of the world to both opportunities and challenges.[25]

Firstly, improvements in communications and transport technologies have significantly lowered the cost of moving information, goods and services across long distances (see

---

25 Lord Sainsbury of Turville, 'The Race to the Top – A Review of Government's Science and Innovation Policies', HM Treasury, 2007.

Chart 3.1). The falling costs of air transport, and major technological advances in transportation such as 'containerisation' and 'intermodal transportation' have significantly lowered the costs and increased the quality of the global transport infrastructure. While geographic distance continues to be important when making decisions about where to produce large, bulky and heavy items like TVs and cars, the falling price of transportation means that more and more products are being sent by air. Notebook computers travel by air from Penang, Malaysia to the United States, and luxurious cashmere sweaters are flown from Xinjiang, China to high-end department stores in Europe and the United States.

Chart 3.1

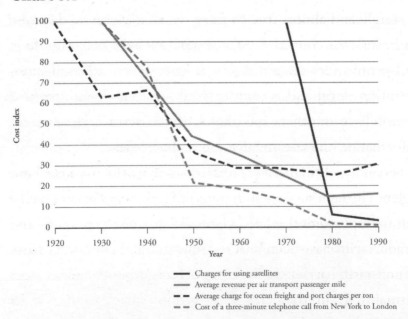

Charges for using satellites
Average revenue per air transport passenger mile
Average charge for ocean freight and port charges per ton
Cost of a three-minute telephone call from New York to London

('The Race to the Top: A Review of Government's Science and Innovation Policies', HM Treasury, 2007.)

These changes have extended the reach of firms, making new markets accessible, and promoted trade based on competitive advantage. The shift away from transporting manufactured goods by ship to transporting them by air, combined with a reduction in the average ocean shipping time from forty days to twenty days, has reduced the tariff equivalent of time costs from 32 per cent to 9 per cent. Reductions in delivery time also increase market responsiveness and allow for improved business practice, such as just-in-time delivery.

In the same way that the national highway system built in the 1950s removed transport barriers in the United States and enabled companies to relocate to lower-wage regions like the South, so the laying of global fibre highways has helped to create a seamless global commercial network and made it simple and almost free to move work that can be digitised to lower-cost countries. As a result, software programming, call-centre services, back-office operations, medical transcription, legal and accounting services can all be provided remotely from other countries through increasingly efficient information and communication technologies.

Secondly, tariff barriers that distort world markets have fallen. Through successive rounds of trade negotiation carried out to implement the 1947 General Agreement on Tariffs and Trade, tariffs have been lowered, quotas eliminated and a mass of non-tariff barriers to the entry of foreign goods and services dismantled. In the 'Uruguay Round' negotiations (1986 to 1994), even deeper cuts were agreed upon, along with the 1994 decision to establish the World Trade Organization.

Since 1988, average applied tariff rates have more than halved in the USA and fallen by over 70 per cent in the EU, and as a result goods and services pour across national borders, and producers everywhere are exposed to competition.

Finally, as the result of the removal of capital controls, the speed with which money flows around the world has increased dramatically in the last thirty-five years. Between 1970 and 2000, cross-border purchases of bonds and equities grew fifty-four times in the United States, fifty-five times in Japan and sixty times in Germany. Companies also increasingly look to foreign markets for equity. Twenty years ago, most companies raised equity through their domestic equity markets. But because of the internationalisation of finance, the proportion of equities raised on foreign markets as a share of global equity issues rose from 10 per cent in 1985 to 27 per cent in 1995. At the same time, the largest European banks reduced their commitments to domestic firms in order to focus on global markets.

As a result of these developments we find that the amount of foreign equity held by American institutional investors increased from US$128.7 billion in 1988 to $1,787 billion in 2000, and the average percentage of total assets held in international equities by the largest twenty-five American pension funds increased from 4.8 per cent in 1991 to 18.00 per cent in 1999. In bank-based financial systems, these developments obviously had the potential to disrupt the supply of patient capital – that is, capital not looking for a quick return – as such institutional investors have tended to have a strong preference for the adoption of shareholder-value practices that maximise return on equity. In France, foreign investors owned 41.29 per cent of the equity capital of CAC 40 firms (the top firms on the French Stock Exchange) in 2001, and in Germany the comparable figure for the Dax 30 companies (the top firms on the German Stock Exchange) in 1999 was 28.5 per cent.

As national controls on the movement of capital across borders were lifted, new opportunities for speculation as well as productive investment began to emerge. Large amounts of money could be moved in and out of countries instantaneously by a hedge fund or a bond trader anywhere in the world. And because no new regulations designed for this situation were introduced, a dangerous new volatility was generated which meant that governments were able to do little to protect their economies when their currencies came under attack, as they did in crises like those in Western Europe (1992), Mexico (1994), Asia (1997), Russia (1998) and Argentina (2002).

Then, in the midst of all this massive change, a vast new group of people walked out onto the economic playing field from China, India and the former Soviet Union. As a result of the collapse of Communism, China's shift to market capitalism and India's dismantling of its command-and-control economy, 1.5 billion new low-paid workers entered the world's labour market, almost exactly doubling it. It can be argued that only 10 per cent of this new group of people had the education and training to compete effectively in the global economy, but 150 million people is roughly the size of the US workforce and it is not possible to bring this number of people into the world economy without it having a major impact.

If we want to understand fully what is happening in the world economy, we should note one other change taking place in parallel with globalisation that is having a major impact on the location of industry. Manufacturing that used to be contained within the four walls of a single factory can now, through the use of digital technologies and improvements in communications and transport, be broken down into modules which can then potentially be distributed around the world. This has produced a fragmentation of the manufacturing chain, with R&D, design, supply management, production, distribution, logistics and the provision of after-sale services all potentially located in different countries.

This fragmentation of manufacturing can speed up the rate of innovation because it is possible to pull together relatively easily combinations of sophisticated components that were invented for quite different purposes. The Apple iPod could move from concept to market in less than a year because it combines components that were already being made by others.

Fragmentation is also a way of specialising and making the most of competitive advantage. UK firms can increase their productivity and reduce prices by outsourcing the parts of their production chain which can more efficiently be located in other parts of the world. The increased productivity of domestic firms is such that it has been found to have positive employment effects that outweigh the initial loss of jobs from outsourcing. At the same time, UK firms can benefit from increased demands for goods and services from firms in other countries looking to outsource parts of their production chain such as business services.

Fragmentation therefore has two important policy implications: first, governments should accept that companies may for competitive reasons have to outsource some part of their manufacturing chain. Second, in every industry we should focus our innovation policies, our inward investment policies and our export promotion policies on those parts of the manufacturing chain where as a country we are most likely to be successful: that is, the knowledge-intensive parts. In many cases this will be R&D and design, and in other cases it will be the production process itself.

There are those who see globalisation only in terms of price competition and who therefore believe that the emergence of low-wage countries will inevitably result in a downward slide of wages, social welfare and environmental practices. They fear that all countries will be involved in a 'race to the bottom', with firms competing by seeking ever-cheaper labour, land and capital, and countries competing by deregulating and shrinking social benefits. But any strategy for developed countries which is based on competing on low wages will end up in a downward spiral, where each year brings a new competitor: today the coastal regions of China, tomorrow the interior of China, or Vietnam and India.

Fortunately, the reality of international competition is very different. A nation's standard of living over a period of years depends on the rate of productivity growth and levels of employment. Productivity in turn depends on the innovativeness and quality of a country's products and on the prices that they can command in the marketplace, as well as on the efficiency with which they can be produced.

For a nation to achieve sustained productivity growth, its firms must continuously increase their organisational and technological capabilities. They must increase their productivity in existing industries by improving product quality, adding new and attractive features, using new product technology and raising production efficiency. And they must develop the capability to compete in new and more sophisticated industries, where productivity is generally higher.

So developed countries should not see themselves as competing with developing countries in a 'race to the bottom', but in a 'race to the top'. In a 'race to the bottom', cheap labour and a 'favourable' exchange rate may be the best way to achieve competitiveness, but in a 'race to the top', the goal for companies must be to develop the products and services that command premium prices in international markets and which can support high wages. Governments need to consider, therefore, how they can provide the best conditions for companies to translate new ideas into new products and services, or new processes and production methods, as it is support for this innovation that will help boost productivity and standards of living.

Developed countries should not think, however, that they have plenty of time to upgrade their economies. Countries like China and India do not intend to stay on the lower rungs of the economic ladder for long, manufacturing cheap products based on low technology, low skills and low wages. They want to raise their standard of living and they understand that to do so they must improve the quality of their goods and services, increase their rate of innovation and move into higher-value-added goods and services.

Firm Capabilities in a Global Economy

While there is almost universal agreement about the forces behind globalisation, there is sharp disagreement over the key issue for political economy raised by globalisation, which is whether heightened competitive pressures will undermine the stability of regulatory regimes and national institutions. Will competitive pressures unleashed by liberalisation and deregulation undermine the institutional differences between countries and drive all economies towards a similar market model?

To these questions, neo-liberalism gives a clear view which flows from its model of capitalism. This model has three important features. Firstly, firms in all countries are seen as essentially similar, and no importance is attached to their different organisational and technological capabilities. Secondly, the unit labour cost of firms is seen as the only competitive issue and it is assumed that firms will, therefore, always move their production abroad if they can find cheaper labour there. And thirdly, when firms threaten to exit the economy because they can lower their costs by going abroad, governments will alter their regulatory frameworks so as to lower domestic labour costs, reduce rates of taxation and reduce the protection of the environment. There will, therefore, inevitably be a 'race to the bottom'.

But in the real world, firms in different countries draw different strengths and weaknesses from the different institutions in their countries and therefore do not respond to globalisation in the same way. An American company such as Apple or Google is born into an environment where capital is likely to come from venture-capital investors and then the stock market; where workers are educated and trained by schools and universities, not by the company; where new skills are acquired by hiring new employees, not retraining old ones; and where labour–management relations are often poor. As a result it is likely, as we shall see in Chapter 5 on the varieties of capitalism, to compete on the basis of radical innovation.

In countries such as the USA, firms faced with greater international competition are likely, therefore, to put pressure on their governments to deregulate their economies, as this will improve their competitiveness. The government will also be sympathetic, as the comparative advantage of the economy as a whole depends on the effectiveness of market mechanisms.

A German firm such as Siemens or BMW, on the other hand, is born into an environment featuring institutions that provide a big role for labour in the governance of companies, good labour–management relationships, financial institutions that have historically provided patient capital through banks rather than through stock markets, and an excellent system of vocational education. As a result, such firms will probably compete on the basis of incremental innovation.

In countries such as Germany, the dynamic unleashed by globalisation is likely, therefore, to be very different. There will, of course, be calls for deregulation in these economies, but firms are less likely to be supportive of them because they know that they draw competitive advantage from the institutions of their country. Governments will also be less sympathetic because deregulation may lead to a reduction in the country's comparative advantage. In these countries we are more likely to see coalitions of firms and workers defending regulatory regimes, which they believe give them a competitive advantage in world markets.

In countries such as Germany, firms will not automatically move their activities offshore when they are offered low-cost labour abroad. Firms will always be attracted by cheaper labour that comes with high levels of skill and productivity, but firms also know that they derive competitive advantages from institutions in their home country and will be reluctant to give these up simply to reduce wage costs.

Increasing flows of trade in recent years do not appear to have erased the institutional differences across nations. But we should not be surprised by this, as world trade has been increasing for fifty years without forcing convergence to take place. If, as I have argued, institutions are an important source of competitive advantage, then we are as likely to see a strengthening of institutional differences as a reduction of them.

What Governments Should Do

The fundamental question that governments of developed countries have to address today is how, in an open international economy which has been flooded with new competitors, they can build a prosperous society with opportunities for all their citizens to do well. I believe that there are two tasks that they need to tackle if they are to build such a society.

Firstly, governments need to maintain broad public support for openness, and for the rapid deployment of resources from one activity to another, by providing social protection for individuals against the risks of globalisation. Secondly, they need to reform their economic institutions to make them effective and, in particular, ensure that they have a world-class national system of innovation so that they can retain the knowledge-intensive activities of their own firms and attract the knowledge-intensive activities of foreign firms. At the same time they should focus their inward investment and export promotion policies on the same activities of firms.

Globalisation is leading to a major restructuring of global economic activity. In 1980, less than a tenth of manufacturing exports came from developing countries; today the figure is almost 30 per cent. China alone is producing 70 per cent of the world's photocopiers, 50 per cent of cameras, 40 per cent of microwaves and 25 per cent of textiles, though as we will see shortly, much of this is being done by foreign-funded enterprises (FFEs). At the same time India is taking huge strides forward in the services sector. At no time since the Industrial

Revolution has the restructuring of global economic activity been so great.

In such a situation there are many people who are right to fear globalisation. Those fears have to do with losing the chance of earning enough through one's best efforts and hard work to support oneself and one's family. Even if there are enormous overall gains to be had from the opening of trade and the integration of the global economy, there is no reason to think that these benefits will be spread across society evenly. The losses of globalisation have been borne disproportionately by some groups in society in the past, and this is likely to be true in the future too.

These fears are likely to lead to calls for protectionism, for maintaining strategic industries at home and for 'level playing fields'. These calls need to be resisted. When we look at the economic growth of developing countries, we will see that a strong case can be made for infant industry protection. But no economic case can be made for the protection of mature declining industries in developed countries. Such protectionism should always be resisted as it will provoke protectionism in others. It is not an escape from change. It is short-sighted, and in the long run leads to greater adjustment costs than if global change is accepted and policies which enable the economy to restructure are implemented. Instead, governments need to develop better policies to provide insurance for individuals against the risks of globalisation, and educational and training opportunities to enable them to gain new well-paying jobs.

The second task which governments of developed countries need to do is to ensure that they have world-class national systems of innovation to retain the knowledge-intensive parts of their own companies and to attract the knowledge-intensive parts of foreign companies. The time has long gone when a low-tax system, a good legal system, a stable government and greenfield sites were enough to retain and attract the knowledge-intensive parts of international companies. International companies now want to know about the presence of world-class research universities, highly skilled workers and high-tech clusters.

A distinction also needs to be made between protecting mature declining industries and stopping the industries of the future being attracted to other countries by large grants, subsidies or tax reductions. In the UK a world-beating company like Rolls-Royce in a key industry of the future is endlessly bombarded with incentives by other countries keen to get it to put its factories or research facilities in their country.

Sometimes the location of its activities abroad will make commercial sense for such a company, but it is short-sighted for the UK government to let other countries attract away our future industries without giving serious thought as to how we can keep them in our country.

Where a foreign company in an industry of the future is looking at locating one of its production facilities or research laboratories in the UK, and their presence would strengthen one of our key industries, we should be prepared to look at what help, financial or otherwise, we can provide to attract them to our country. Economists will argue that it is impossible to make a distinction between such cases and the protection of mature declining industries, but a simple and excellent test is whether such help leads to an acceleration of industrial change or retards it. If it accelerates industrial change, we should do everything we can to support it.

Finally, pessimists about technological advance and employment will say that, although the many predictions since the Industrial Revolution about productivity gains and automation reducing the stock of jobs have proved to be wrong, maybe we *are* now faced with such a situation. We should, therefore, protect our current jobs rather than seek to create new, higher-value-added ones. It is, of course, impossible to predict exactly where in the future the new jobs will emerge, but in the UK today, for example, it is possible to see many opportunities for British industries to create new products and services and new industries in areas as diverse as aerospace, pharmaceuticals, plant biotechnology, regenerative medicine, telemedicine, nanotechnology, the space industry, intelligent transport systems, new sources of energy, creative industries, computer games, business and financial services, computer services and education.

Staying Ahead of China

If China was content to remain the low-cost manufacturer of the world, then its emergence as a world economic power would not present too great a challenge to the West. But being the world's low-cost manufacturer is not a position in which any country wants to remain long term, as it depends on its workers being paid extremely low wages and as a result having a low standard of living. The Chinese, therefore, are determined that their firms should continuously accumulate high-level organisational and technological capabilities, and they appear to understand better than some Western governments that they are involved in a 'race to the top' and not a 'race to the bottom'.

While China has achieved huge trade surpluses with the USA, the value added has flowed largely to foreign rather than Chinese companies, except for a small number of gigantic state-owned enterprises. Foreign-funded enterprises (FFEs) accounted for 55 per cent of China's exports in 2003, and in advanced industrial exports the dominance of foreign firms is even greater. Exports of computer equipment shot up from $716 million in 1993 to $41 billion in 2003, with the share of FFEs rising from 74 per cent to 92 per cent.[26] And exports of cellular telephones and laptops, for example, have less than 10 per cent Chinese content, and foreign-funded factories account for most of it, the rest of the hardware and software being imported. China today is not so much the manufacturing centre of the world as its assembly plant.

The Chinese government also understands that any significant increase in the wages of Chinese workers will make China's low-tech exports uncompetitive and mean that

---

26   George J. Gilboy, 'The Myth Behind China's Miracle', *Foreign Affairs*, July / August 2004.

their manufacture will move to countries such as Indonesia, Malaysia, Thailand and Vietnam. If they are going to keep their economy growing at 9 per cent per annum and wages rising, which they need to do to maintain their political credibility, they have to find a way to enable Chinese companies to develop, manufacture and export advanced products.

The Chinese government has therefore embarked on a major programme to boost its national system of innovation.[27] This has a number of features.

Firstly, they are investing heavily in R&D. Over the past decade China has increased its R&D expenditures by about 21 per cent a year, and it now plans to increase its R&D expenditures from the current level of 1.7 per cent of GDP to 2.5 per cent of GDP by 2020. (The US figure in 2004 was 2.7 per cent and the UK 1.8 per cent.) It also plans to introduce unique technical standards that will reduce its dependence on imported technologies by 30 per cent, and to become one of the world's top five economies according to the number of patents and scientific papers published.

To achieve these goals it offers, among other things, tax incentives including accelerated depreciation of investments in R&D facilities and tax breaks on returns from venture capital investments in technology-based start-ups. Special funding also supports the development of domestic technologies that can replace imported ones, and it has tailored procurement

---

27 Thomas Hout and Pankaj Ghemawat, 'China vs. The World – Whose Technology Is It?', *Harvard Business Review*, December 2010.

policies to favour technologies developed domestically. This occurs especially in cities such as Beijing, Shanghai and Guangzhou, where the state wants technology-rich industries to replace low- and mid-tech ones that are moving inland in search of lower wages.

Finally, the Chinese government is forcing multinational companies, in exchange for current and future business opportunities, to form joint ventures with its national champions, transfer the latest technology to them and make a high proportion of their products locally. Mandatory joint ventures, forced technology transfers and local-content requirements are not new elements in Asian development strategies. Japan, South Korea and India, for example, have used them. But the Chinese government is pursuing them particularly aggressively.

As well as these policies to support technology generation and the transfer of technology from abroad, China has also invested massively in education and drawn systematically on its diaspora in order to aid its firms' accumulation of organisational and technological capabilities. As a result of the Cultural Revolution, China froze its higher education sector between 1966 and 1976. But starting in the late 1990s China has undertaken a massive expansion of its tertiary education system to make up for the havoc wreaked on its educational system in the past. As a result, by 2005 its enrolment rate had risen to 19 per cent.

China has also benefited hugely from sending many students abroad for tertiary-level education and training. In 2005, more than 16 per cent of the 2.7 million tertiary students studying outside their home country were from China (not counting Hong Kong). This was a policy initiated after the Cultural Revolution by Deng Xiaoping, when China realised that it had fallen badly behind in science and technology. He gathered together some Chinese scientists living in the UK and America and asked them what he should do. They advised him that China should allow its students to go abroad to study science and do research, and this he agreed to do, in spite of the reservations of senior Communists who thought that China would lose some of its best young people as a result.

It turned out, however, to be a brilliant decision, and a very important way to tap into global knowledge. Not only were the students taught science and technology at some of the best universities in America and Europe, but many of them then did research at these world-class institutions, and some went on to work in high-technology firms. And many of them are now returning to China because of the increasing opportunities and attractive incentive programmes designed to bring them back.

China has also drawn systematically on its diaspora. More than half of the foreign direct investment (FDI) in China has come from Taiwan, Hong Kong and Singapore. Firms from these countries initially moved their more labour-intensive operations into the country. Then as China moved up the technology ladder, they moved more technology-intensive operations into the country. China has also set up special high-technology parks specifically targeted at attracting back experienced overseas Chinese to set up high-tech companies.

These initiatives are now producing results, but China has some way to go before its firms make innovation a core competence and the basis of strategy. We should not be surprised that this is the case. For all its long history up till the overthrow of the Qing dynasty in 1911, China was an absolutist state. Decades of civil war, the Second World War and, in 1949, the Communist Revolution followed. As a result, when Deng Xiaoping started moving China towards a capitalist economy in 1978 it had none of the capitalist institutions that enable people to take the risk of transacting business with other people even if they are strangers, and which are the essential foundation of a capitalist economy. It was only in March 2007, after fourteen years of debate, that the party congress approved new laws protecting individual property rights.[28]

As a result, China's private sector has largely comprised family businesses, or at least personally owned and dominated businesses, the model for which was brought to China by members of the 50 million ethnic Chinese who live around the borders of the South China Sea, mainly refugees from China over the last century and a half. These are small and medium enterprises (SMEs) who use their *guanxi* connections – that is, their personal networks of trust – to make up for China's lack of capitalist institutions.

In manufacturing, their natural skills for networking have allowed them to transcend their scale limitations and build

---

28   Gordon Redding and Michael A. Witt, *The Future of Chinese Capitalism: Choices and Chances*, Oxford University Press, 2007.

industrial competence via the integration of separately owned units in components supply, sub-assembly and assembly. By this means, over a wide range of industries they have come to dominate the world's use of original equipment manufacturers (OEMs) – that is, companies that manufacture products on order from brand-name firms but do not themselves develop brands or new designs. Innovation is not a competitive strength and they do not benefit from strong property rights, good domestic sources of technology or a sophisticated venture-capital industry.

China also remains a fragmented federal system, with the Chinese Communist Party (CCP) controlling all aspects of organised life, including industry associations. Although market reforms have brought more rules to the economy, CCP officials still exercise wide discretion in defining and implementing these rules at a local level. As a result, Chinese managers in the private sector, which now accounts for about two-thirds of the economy, tend to focus on short-term profits, local autonomy and building relationships with CCP officials. If it is to overcome its technological and economic weaknesses, the Chinese government will need to undertake a further programme of economic and political reform.

It would be foolish, however, for the West not to assume that the Chinese will solve the problems they face. If we want to stay ahead of China in the 'race to the top' we will have to abandon the neo-liberal ideology which has paralysed our thinking for the last thirty-five years. We will not be able to compete against China by opening a few more enterprise zones, removing health and safety regulations or reducing the top rate of tax for CEOs.

It is important that we do not introduce regulations unless they significantly improve the effectiveness of an institution at a reasonable cost. It is also important that we do not demotivate our entrepreneurs with high taxes, but there is no evidence to suggest that the removal of a few regulations or a small change in tax rates will lead to a surge of innovation and economic growth.

What we in the West need to do is to make sure that our financial and labour market institutions are working efficiently, that the governance of our companies is effective, that we have world-class national systems of innovation, and that our education and training systems produce the highly skilled workers our industries need. We can be winners in the 'race to the top', but only if we rapidly and systematically reform our economic institutions.

FOUR

A NEW PROGRESSIVE POLITICAL ECONOMY

In the previous two chapters we have seen that economic growth is greatly affected by the impact that four types of economic institutions have on the economic performance of firms in their home countries. These institutions are their financial and labour markets, the governance and management of their firms, their national systems of innovation and their education and training systems. This finding conforms with the defining belief of Progressive political economy that capitalism is a socio-economic system in which institutions play an important role.

To develop a new Progressive political economy, we need to deploy two further defining beliefs of Progressive thinking. Firstly, that the institutions of a country have to be constructed and adapted to changing circumstances by the state because they involve conflicts of interest and create winners and losers and, secondly, that in constructing its economic institutions the state should seek to achieve a fair distribution of wealth as well as economic growth.

The Role of the State

In looking at the role of the state we need first to understand that economic institutions are man-made, though they are not always treated as such. Financial and labour markets in an economy are often treated as natural phenomena and not man-made institutions. 'The market primacy assumption', as Ha-Joon Chang has called it,[29] claims that in the beginning there were markets and that only later did man-made institutions emerge, but this is not historically correct, and markets should be seen as institutions which have to be socially constructed.

A feature of neo-classical economics is the neglect of the institutional arrangements which govern the process of exchange. This is not surprising, however, in an economic theory where there are no transaction costs, as in such a theory markets have no function to perform. In reality, in order for a market transaction to take place, complex institutional arrangements need to exist to enable buyer and seller to make contact, to conduct negotiations to agree the price and terms, to draw up a contract, to carry out any necessary inspection of the goods to establish that they are what they are said to be, and to settle any disputes. If the institutional

---

29   Ha-Joon Chang, *Globalisation, Economic Development and the Role of the State*, Zed Books Ltd, 2003.

arrangements are deficient, then the market will not perform its function efficiently.

As the economist Ronald Coase has written:

> The time has surely gone in which economists could analyse in great detail two individuals exchanging nuts for berries on the edge of the forest and then feel that their analysis of the process of exchange was complete, illuminating though this analysis may be in certain respects. The process of contracting needs to be studied in a real-world setting. We would then learn of the problems that are encountered and how they are overcome, and we would certainly become aware of the richness of the institutional alternatives between which we have to choose.[30]

It is also important to understand that market institutions are based on specific rights/obligations structures which are imposed on the different participants in a particular market and, in the case of externalities, on non-participants as well. The different participants in a market will have different views as to what these rights/obligations should be, and as a result the form that they take has to be decided and enforced by the state as part of the political process. If we use the term 'free market' to describe a market free of government regulations and social control, no such thing exists.

---

30 R. H. Coase, 'The Institutional Structure of Production', *The American Economic Review*, Vol. 82, No. 4 (Sept 1992), pp. 713–19.

This point can be illustrated by looking at the list that Ha-Joon Chang has compiled of the many ways that institutions support markets.[31] As he has pointed out, many of these institutions are not seen as interventions by the state because the rights/obligations structures which underline them have come to be widely accepted. The first way that institutions support markets is by regulating who can participate in them. Children under a certain age will not be allowed to participate in the labour market, and a stock market's listing rules will determine who can participate in it.

Secondly, institutions determine the legitimate objects of market exchange. For example, laws will make it illegal to create a market for addictive drugs, 'indecent publications', human organs or firearms. Thirdly, institutions define the rights and obligations of the participants. For example, zoning laws, environmental laws regarding pollution or noise and fire regulations will define how property rights can be exercised, while health and safety laws and employment laws will define the rights and obligations of workers and employers. Fourthly, institutions play a key role in regulating the process of exchange itself. For example, there are in most countries regulations regarding fraud, breach of contract, default and bankruptcy, and consumer and liability laws specify how and when buyers of unsatisfactory or faulty products can return them or claim compensation.

---

31 Ha-Joon Chang, 'The Market, the State and Institutions in Economic Development' in Ha-Joon Chang (ed.), *Rethinking Development Economics*, Anthem Press, 2003.

It is also important to understand that the institutions which support markets are not forms of spontaneous order. Nor do they embody some structure of supposed fundamental rights. Market institutions are human artefacts created in all their varieties beyond the most simple by the state, and ultimately they all need to be justified by their contribution to the well-being of society and to be perpetually open to reform.

When Mrs Thatcher radically changed employment law in the 1980s in the UK, she did not return the market to some natural state, but instead drastically altered the rights/obligations structure of employers and trade unions in the labour market. Whatever the rights and wrongs of the radical action she took, it would be incorrect to portray it as a case of returning the market to some natural state.

If we turn now to the second of the four institutions which impact on the rate of economic growth, namely, the governance and management of firms, it is easy once again to fall into the trap of thinking of them as natural phenomena, when in reality they are social constructions which have changed their form almost continuously over the centuries.

In the Middle Ages we see the emergence of 'bodies corporate', that is, towns, universities and guilds which had a life beyond that of their members. In the sixteenth and seventeenth centuries, European monarchs created chartered companies, such as the East India Company and the Virginia Company, to trade abroad. But it was in nineteenth-century Britain that a series of Company Acts finally brought together the three big ideas behind the modern company: that it could be an 'artificial person' with the same ability to do business as a real person, that it could issue tradeable shares to any number of investors and that those investors could have limited liability.

The fact that firms are social constructions is shown by the controversy that surrounded their creation. Adam Smith derided joint-stock companies with limited liability as antiquated and inefficient, and the Victorian thinker A.V. Dicey, was worried that they would bring in a new age of collectivism. Victorian liberals were also doubtful that professional managers could be trusted to act in the interest of the owner-shareholders. They were right to be concerned about this point, and the potential conflict between the 'principals' who own companies and their 'agents' who run them, as we shall see later on, is still a major issue. The political economist John Stuart Mill was only able to put to rest his concerns about joint-stock companies by deciding that for new capital-hungry businesses, like railways, the only alternative to them was direct state control.

A country's national system of innovation and its education and training system are also obviously man-made institutions. Neither institution emerges spontaneously in an economy, and they can both take a number of forms depending on the economic views of those who design them.

Neo-liberals would like to believe that a country's economic institutions start up and evolve spontaneously, without any involvement of the state, but Progressive thinkers believe the state has to play a key role in two sets of institutions. The first set consists of the regulations which govern the commercial relationships of individuals and firms. The most important of these are the regulations which govern financial and labour markets, and the behaviour of firms. As a result of these regulations, when a person joins a company as an employee or buys a share, he knows what rights and obligations he takes on as a result.

These institutions have to be constructed, and adapted to changing circumstances, by the state because the participants affected have different interests and because the way they are drawn up creates winners and losers. While rules covering economic activities can be drawn up by small groups of people who trust each other, for the full benefits of capitalism to be achieved the state has to draw up the regulations which enable people to take the risk of transacting business with anyone within reason. Such regulations lead to an exponential increase in the total volume of business that a single individual can initiate and handle, and dramatically increase national wealth.

The second set of economic institutions consists of the organisations which provide the public goods resources which industry needs in order to build competitive advantage. These consist mainly of a country's national system of innovation and its education and training system, and have to be funded largely by the state. Both sets of economic institutions should be seen as the 'soft infrastructure of capitalism', and as public goods which only the state can provide.

It is important to understand, however, that the role of the state is an enabling or market-supporting one, not the command-and-control role promoted by traditional socialists or the minimalist role which is the goal of neo-liberals. The role of the state is not to override markets or neglect them, but to make certain that the incentives for market participants serve to align their actions with the function the market is required to perform. The talents of individual entrepreneurs are vitally important for the achievement of economic growth, but it requires economic institutions to enable entrepreneurs to have access to the research and skilled people they need to be successful.

It is also a central argument of this book that the market-supporting economic institutions of the enabling state, rather than the market-directing economic institutions found in the command-and-control state or the weak institutions of the minimal state, are the ones that lead to faster economic growth. Market-supporting economic institutions incentivise the great mass of people to create wealth by using their talents and skills, and give them a fair share of the resulting wealth. This involves secure private property, an absence of monopolies, an unbiased system of law, regulations to prevent theft and fraud, taxation only with democratic consent, and effective national systems of innovation and education and training.

Market-directing economic institutions, such as are found in absolutist monarchies, Communist states and the southern states of America up until the 1960s, limit the choices that people can make while invariably allowing a powerful elite to appropriate much of the wealth created. They limit the companies that people can set up and the jobs they can do, and they lay down the wages that people get for particular jobs and the prices at which goods can be sold. The minimal state, on the other hand, by leaving great gaps in the regulatory system, allows people to be exploited by groups who have power or access to information not available to everyone.

If market-supporting economic institutions are the source of economic growth, why then do not all countries adopt them? The answer lies in politics and political institutions. Politics and political institutions are the process by which a society chooses the rules that will govern it. Political institutions include not only written constitutions and whether a society is a democracy, but also how political power is distributed in a society, particularly the ability of different groups to act collectively, and a country will not develop or adopt the market-supporting economic institutions that are best for economic growth and the welfare of its citizens if an elite controls the country's politics and political institutions, and believes that market-directing economic institutions best serve its interests.

Economic growth that is produced by market-supporting economic institutions creates winners and losers, and is accompanied by 'creative destruction'. This creates new sectors which attract resources away from the old, creates new firms which take business away from established ones and develops new technologies which make existing skills and machines obsolete. And in turn, the economic winners in this process create winners and losers in the political arena. A fear of 'creative destruction', therefore, causes political elites to oppose economic growth.

Economic Growth and the Rise of Capitalist Institutions

Having described the role of the state in our new, institutionalist political economy, we now need to see whether history, the only laboratory available to economists, provides us with any evidence that this is a more realistic model than the neo-liberal one which many countries have embraced in recent years. We cannot do controlled laboratory experiments which can be replicated, and in which the experimenter directly manipulates variables, as is done in laboratory physical sciences and molecular biology, but we can look back at the natural experiments of history and see whether, in those cases where the economic performance of a country greatly improved, growth was accompanied by a change in economic institutions.

If we do so, and if we look at the pattern of world prosperity and inequality which has emerged since the late eighteenth century and the Industrial Revolution in England, we find a considerable amount of evidence which supports an institutionalist view of political economy. As Paul Bairoch has shown, before the Industrial Revolution the income gap between the poorest and the richest country was certainly smaller than the ratio 1.0 to 2.0 and probably of the order of only 1.0 to 1.5.[32]

---

32   Paul Bairoch, 'The Main Trends in National Economic Disparities since the Industrial Revolution' in Paul Bairoch and Maurice Levy-Laboyer (eds), *Disparities in Economic Development since the Industrial Revolution*, Macmillan, 1981.

Thereafter, there was a sharp difference in the economic performance of different countries, so that today there are huge differences in the incomes and standards of living of rich and poor countries in the world. The average per capita income in sub-Saharan Africa today, for example, is less than one-twentieth of that in the United States. And if we look at each case where the economic growth of a country took off, we consistently find a change in the country's economic institutions.

If we look first at the late eighteenth century, the most dynamic economies were the Netherlands and England, both of which were benefiting from the abolition or withering away of feudal institutions. The Netherlands was probably the European society least affected by feudal institutions such as serfdom, and its guilds were weak. In 1568 it had also revolted against Spanish rule and organised itself as a republic.

England, on the other hand, was the country where feudal institutions collapsed earliest. Serfdom had vanished by 1500, guilds lost their power in the sixteenth and seventeenth centuries, and the church was expropriated and its land sold off by Henry VIII in the 1530s. At the beginning of the seventeenth century, however, the economy was still choked by domestic and international monopolies. In 1621 there were 700 domestic monopolies covering everything from coal, soap, dyes and butter to writing paper and printed books. The ability to grant monopolies was a key source of revenue for the state and was often used as a way of granting exclusive rights to the supporters of the King. Most land was also covered by archaic forms of property rights that made it impossible to sell and risky to invest in, and the state engaged in arbitrary taxation and abused the legal system.

All this changed after the Civil War between 1642 and 1651 and the Glorious Revolution of 1688.[33] As a result of these political upheavals, the power of the King and the executive was restricted, and the power to determine economic institutions was handed over to Parliament. As a result the second half of the seventeenth century in England saw the emergence of the market-supporting institutions of capitalism.

The government enforced property rights, including granting property rights for ideas, and provided as a result a major stimulus for innovation. Arbitrary taxation ceased and monopolies were abolished almost completely. Property rights were rationalised, which facilitated the construction of infrastructure, particularly the roads, canals and later the railways that would be crucial for industrial growth. The English state also strongly supported the country's mercantile activities by using the full power of the English Navy, and promoted textile production by protecting it from foreign imports.

There was one other significant change in institutions that emerged from the Glorious Revolution. This was the continuation of the process of political centralisation that had been started by the Tudor kings. Parliament had opposed making the state more effective and better resourced prior to 1688

---

33 Daron Acemoglu and James A. Robinson, *Why Nations Fail – The Origins of Power, Prosperity and Poverty*, Profile Books, 2012.

because it could not control it, but after 1688 it was a different matter. The capability and capacity of the state increased, with expenditure soon reaching around 10 per cent of national income. This was a very large state budget for the period, and is in fact larger than what we see today in many parts of the world.

By 1760, the combination of all these factors began to have an effect. There was a jump in the number of patented inventions. The number of patents sealed had been about eighty in the period 1740–49. In the period 1750–59 it increased to over 100, and to nearly 300 in the period 1770–79. Patents are an imperfect indicator of innovation, but there were no changes in this period in the way they were granted which might invalidate the series. There was also a burst of technological change as inventors such as James Watt, the perfector of the steam engine, and Richard Arkwright, the inventor of the water frame for spinning, were able to take up the economic opportunities generated by their ideas, knowing that the institutions existed to enable them to make and sell profitably the products based on their ideas.

A stream of innovations revolutionised spinning. In 1769, Arkwright patented his water frame. This was complemented by Hargreaves's invention in 1764 of the spinning jenny, which was further developed by Samuel Crompton into the 'mule', and later by Richard Roberts into the 'self-acting mule'. The impact of this stream of innovations was immense. In the eighteenth century, Indian hand spinners took 50,000 operative hours to process 100 lb of cotton. Crompton's mule took 2,000 operative hours to process the same amount of cotton, while Roberts' automatic mule took 135 hours. This is what is meant when one talks about the acquisition by firms of organisational and technological capabilities and the creation of wealth.

The institutionalist political economy put forward in this book also explains much better than geography or culture the pattern of economic growth and inequality across the world which has emerged since the late eighteenth century and the Industrial Revolution in England. It explains why Western European nations and their colonial offshoots, filled with European settlers, started growing in the nineteenth century, why Russia and Austria-Hungry failed to do so, and why Japan's economy improved dramatically after the Meiji Restoration of 1868. It also explains why some countries have remained disastrously poor.

The reason that Western European nations and their 'settler colonies' such as Australia, Canada and the United States were able, with a time lag, to achieve a similar growth to Great Britain is that they followed a similar path to the long struggle in England against the monarchy. This led to centralised states with pluralistic political institutions, and in time to market-supporting institutions and industrialisation. In the case of Russia and Austria-Hungary, on the other hand, they not only maintained market-directing institutions but also blocked new technologies and the basic investments in infrastructure which might bring them into the country. They did this because they believed that such changes would lead to political instability.

A great deal of intellectual energy has been expended in explaining why the Japanese economy grew so strongly after the Second World War, but the most important change in Japan's economic fortunes took place in 1868 with the Meiji Restoration. Japan was then an economically underdeveloped country that had been controlled since 1603 by the Tokugawa family, the dominant member of a class of feudal lords. Society was divided into castes – samurai, peasants, artisans and merchants – and the country was divided into several hundred domains ruled by lords called *daimyo*. Draconian restrictions on international trade and contacts also existed. As a result of these institutions, Japan was poor.

Then in 1853, four US warships, commanded by Matthew C. Perry, entered Edo Bay, demanding trade concessions similar to those that England obtained from the Chinese in the Opium Wars. Partly in response to the national vulnerability this demonstrated, in 1868 the Tokugawa family was overthrown and the Emperor Meiji came to power. This led to a massive transformation of Japan's institutions.

The new regime undertook major reforms. All of the feudal domains were 'surrendered' to the Emperor. The four orders of society and the restrictions on internal migration and trade were abolished. The peasants were confirmed in the ownership of their land and modern property rights were created. In 1872, elementary schooling was made compulsory, and in 1890 a written constitution was adopted that created a constitutional monarch. It was impossible, however, for Japan to use tariffs to promote industrial development because the maximum tariff was capped at 5.0 per cent by a treaty forced on Japan by the Western powers in 1866. Japan recovered control over its tariffs in 1894 and 1911, and they were immediately raised to protect industry. As a result of all these changes, per capita GDP increased impressively from $737 in 1870 to $2,874 in 1940.

Finally, history teaches us that a strong state able to build and enforce the market-supporting institutions of capitalism is an essential pre-condition of economic development. The freest, most neo-liberal states in the world are not the United States or Hong Kong, but 'failed states' such as Afghanistan, Somalia and the Congo where no group of warlords is sufficiently dominant to form a government.

The natural experiments of history provide us, then, with a great deal of evidence that the institutionalist political economy set out in this book is a more realistic model of how the economy works than the neo-liberal one which many people have embraced in recent years. In this model, the state has a key role to play in the economy in addition to its macroeconomic responsibilities. It is, however, an enabling role which is based on pluralistic political institutions rather than the command-and-control role which we find in absolutist monarchies and Communist economies, or the weak role of the minimalist state which is championed by neo-liberals.

Enterprise and Social Justice

If we see the state as performing a key role in the economy, this inevitably raises the question of how we measure its performance. Neo-liberals assess the performance of an economy simply in terms of economic growth and freedom. But this is clearly unsatisfactory. There are very few people concerned with the well-being of society who would seriously argue that a wealthy society where most of the wealth is held by the top 1 per cent of the population is a better society than a slightly less wealthy society where the wealth is more evenly spread.

At the same time, there is clearly a trade-off between wealth creation and a simple egalitarian view of social justice. A society in which there are no rewards for hard work and enterprise will certainly be a poorer one. The difficulty which this trade-off poses for politicians and policy-makers was well expressed by Robert Reich when he wrote: 'Prosperity for some at the cost of dire poverty for others is morally offensive. Equality at the price of stagnation has no greater appeal.'[34]

To deal with this issue, most Progressive political economists have felt the need to introduce some measure of social justice when looking at the performance of different economic systems. The measure chosen by many socialist economists in the past, like Tony Crosland in *The Future of Socialism*, is equality.[35] However, in retrospect this has not proved useful as a measure of success for politicians and policy-makers trying to improve the well-being of their societies. The reasons are threefold. Firstly, it is extremely difficult to devise

---

34   Robert B. Reich, 'The Democrats' Promise of Prosperity' in Robert E. Levin (ed.), *Democratic Blueprints*, Hippocrene Books, 1988.

35   Anthony Crosland, *The Future of Socialism*, Jonathan Cape, 1956.

practical and effective policies to achieve equality of incomes in a market economy. The only two policies which have been tried are redistribution based on extremely high tax rates, and the setting of wage and salary levels by government. Trials of both these policies, however, have rapidly descended into bureaucratic nightmares as well as leading to distorted economic incentives.

Secondly, there is undoubtedly a huge trade-off between equality and economic growth. Egalitarianism fails to recognise the fundamental truth that virtually all the wealth in a modern society is the result of human action and not an endowment from heaven. The egalitarian idea that production and distribution are separable activities is based on the delusion that human action will proceed as before if it is unlinked from a system of rewards. It is also difficult to approve of a system which, if it could be achieved, would extinguish any sense of human responsibility, and in practice egalitarian policies tend to generate a corrupt, inefficient and exploitative parallel economy.

Thirdly, it appears that egalitarianism is not a popular policy even for many poor people. The great majority of people are happy to see entrepreneurs well rewarded provided that they feel that they have made a real contribution to the economy and the rewards are proportionate. Equally, they are not happy to see lazy or incompetent workers given the same rewards as skilled workers who put in long hours. All too often in the past, left-of-centre political parties have preached the virtues of egalitarianism while in opposition and then have found themselves unable to come up with any credible policies for the distribution of wealth when in government.

A much more useful way of looking at the distribution of wealth, as Will Hutton has argued, is social justice defined as fairness.[36] Again there are three reasons for holding this view. Firstly, it is much easier to devise policies to achieve this goal than it is to achieve equality of outcomes. For example, policies have been devised to give people more equal life chances and to diminish social inheritance. This covers both educational policies and policies to reduce the impact of child poverty. I see social mobility as one of the key measures of a fair society, and the policies of government can make a huge difference. In Denmark, for example, the impact of a father's education on a child's secondary school attainment has disappeared altogether in the youngest cohort. Schemes of social insurance to protect people during periods of illness and unemployment are also important as ways of increasing fairness.

But today, arguably the area which requires most attention is what Jacob Hacker has called policies of 'pre-distribution';[37] that is, the way in which the market distributes its rewards in the first place. As we saw in Chapter 1, the increase in inequality in countries such as the USA and Great Britain in recent years was largely the result of huge increases in the

---

36   Will Hutton, Essay on 'Liberal Social Democracy, Fairness and Good Capitalism', produced for the Progressive Governance Conference, Oslo, 2011.

37   Jacob S. Hacker, Essay on 'The Institutional Foundations of Middle-Class Democracy', produced for the Progressive Governance Conference, Oslo, 2011.

rewards of those who work in financial markets and the pay of top business executives. These changes were mainly due not to 'skill-based technological change' but to major changes taking place in financial markets.

The large sums of money flowing through Wall Street and financial deregulation resulted in ever-larger amounts of money being creamed off by traders, salesmen and bankers. From 1948 until 1979, average compensation in the banking sector was essentially the same as in the private sector overall. Then it shot up, with the result that in 2007 the average bank employee earned almost twice as much as the average private sector worker.

Analysing compensation in the financial sector, Thomas Philippon and Ariell Reshef found that the 'excess relative wage' in finance – that is, the amount which could not be explained by differences in education level and job security – went from zero around 1980 to over 40 percentage points by 2006.[38] They also produced the chart below (Chart 4.1) which shows over the period 1910 to 2010 the ratio between average wages in finance and the average wages in the private sector, and their estimate of financial deregulation. This chart suggests both that institutional change, in this case financial deregulation, can have a significant impact on the distribution of income, and that those increases in income which do

---

38 Thomas Philippon and Ariell Reshef, 'Wages and Human Capital in the US Financial Industry: 1909–2006', (Working paper, December 2008).

not reflect a greater contribution to wealth creation can be corrected by economic reform.

Chart 4.1 Relative Financial Wages and Financial Deregulation

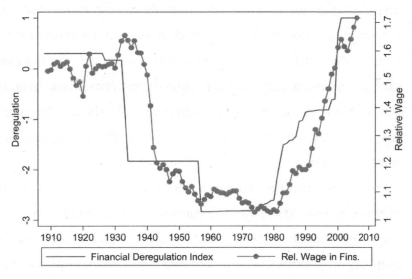

(Thomas Philippon and Ariell Reshef, 'Wages and Human Capital in the US Financial Industry: 1909–2006', Working Paper, December 2008.)

The increase in the pay of top business executives, on the other hand, was largely due, as we shall see in Chapter 6, to the rise of investment managers in the investment chain and their failure to exercise their rights as shareholders to control the compensation of top business executives. A simplistic application of the powerful idea of financial-markets-based compensation – that is, linking the pay of executives to the share price of their company – also had a major impact.

These increases were not due, therefore, to any increase

in the contribution of these two groups to the economy, but were payments creamed off from the returns to savers. They were essentially due to two institutional failures, and I will show in Chapter 6 how they can be rectified.

The second reason for preferring social justice, defined as fairness, as a goal for the distribution of wealth is that, far from it involving a trade-off with economic growth, it is likely to increase prosperity. Improving the education and skills of children from poor families, increasing the willingness of people to change jobs by protecting them and retraining them during periods of unemployment, as the Danish system of flexi-security does, and reducing the rewards of wealth appropriation as opposed to wealth creation, are all ways of increasing economic growth rather than diminishing it.

The final reason for preferring social justice, defined as fairness, is that it reflects the values of many people in our societies. What angers people is not the huge rewards that entrepreneurs receive when they have taken great risks and built up new businesses, but the huge rewards that executives take away when they have failed or when the performance of their companies has been no better than average. Also, people rightly believe that the vast rewards that financial executives receive are not justified by the contribution they make to economic growth.

We also see this sense of social justice, defined as fairness, in other situations. As Will Hutton has pointed out, the rise of single-issue parties and political groupings in Europe – the English Defence League, True Finns, the Italian Northern

League, the Dutch Freedom Party or the Danish *Folkeparti* — organised in varying degrees in response to the increase of immigrants in their countries, cannot be explained by saying that Europe has become more xenophobic or racist than it used to be. Those parties have come into existence in response to a sense of injustice felt by many poor people. Immigrants are seen as having immediate access to schools, housing and healthcare without having contributed to them, and this offends many people's sense of fairness.

If Progressive politicians and policy-makers adopt the above view of political economy, it also has the advantage that it enables them to argue for policies that are based on both responsibility and fairness. The standard of living that a person achieves, they can say, will largely depend on that person's own efforts, but at the same time people will not start their careers burdened by huge disadvantages or be allowed during their careers to appropriate the wealth of others.

What went wrong in the run-up to the financial crash of 2008, and what needs to be put right, was set out by Barack Obama, then a Presidential candidate, in a campaign speech on 27 March 2008:

> We've lost some of that sense of shared prosperity. Now, this loss has not happened by accident. It's because of decisions made in boardrooms, on trading floors and in Washington. Under Republican and Democratic administrations, we've failed to guard against practices that all too often rewarded financial manipulation instead of productivity and sound

business practice. We let the special interests put their thumbs on the economic scales.

The American economy does not stand still and neither should the rules that govern it ... Unfortunately, instead of establishing a 21st-century regulatory framework, we simply dismantled the old one, aided by a legal but corrupt bargain in which campaign money all too often shaped policy and watered down oversight. In doing so we encouraged a winner-take-all, anything-goes environment that helped foster devastating dislocations in our economy.

A New Progressive Political Economy

The new Progressive political economy which I have set out in this chapter is different from neo-liberal political economy because it reflects three key beliefs of Progressive thinkers. It is based on the beliefs that capitalism is a socio-economic system in which institutions play an important role, and that the state has to build and reform those institutions, and it judges the performance of economies in terms of economic growth, freedom and social justice.

I believe that J. M. Keynes was right when he wrote: 'The political problem of mankind is to combine three things: Economic efficiency, social justice and individual liberty.'[39] There are neo-liberals who will argue that freedom and social justice are incompatible, but unless one believes that people have a fundamental freedom not to pay taxes or a fundamental

---

39   J. M. Keynes, 'Politics', in *Essays in Persuasion*, Macmillan, 1931.

freedom to appropriate the wealth of their fellow citizens, there is no incompatibility between freedom and fairness.

I also believe that the Progressive political economy I have described is based on a more realistic model of how the economy works. It doesn't only focus on the allocation of capital and labour in the economy, but also puts firms and entrepreneurs at the centre of the economy and focuses on their accumulation of organisational and technological capabilities. In addition, it recognises that institutions play a large role in the economy, as opposed to the institution-free world of neo-liberalism. For these reasons it is of much greater value to politicians and policy-makers trying to improve the well-being of their societies.

Economic reform also plays a different role in Progressive political economy as compared with neo-liberal political economy. In a Progressive political economy, economic reform involves creating new institutions as well as changing and abolishing old ones, while in neo-liberalism, economic reform is seen always in terms of removing regulations and reducing the role of the state.

This last point has considerable importance for policy-making and can be illustrated by looking at market reform in three very different situations: incremental reforms designed to enhance the efficiency of markets in advanced industrial countries; market reform in countries making the transition from a command-and-control economy to a market economy; and market reform in developing countries.

If we look first at advanced industrial countries, the

deregulation debate of the last thirty-five years assumed a zero-sum relationship between government and markets: that is to say, fewer regulations automatically mean more market competition. But the relationship is more complicated than that. If one wants to maximise competition then one needs to remove market-directing regulations that impede it, such as price and entry restrictions, but at the same time one usually needs to increase market-supporting regulations, which put in place a more sophisticated market infrastructure, more regulations to sustain an antitrust policy and more regulations to protect society from negative externalities, including health, safety and environmental regulations.

As Steven K. Vogel has pointed out, the deregulation movement did not cut back regulation and produce more competition, but produced freer markets and more rules.[40] So, for example, the Thatcher reforms in the UK led to the creation of no fewer than twelve new regulatory agencies, and Britain's 'Big Bang' financial liberalisation of 1986 was accompanied by the passage of the Financial Services Act, which brought in a far more extensive, intrusive and legalistic regulatory regime. This is an important point because it means that market reform is not simply about liberating markets from government control but about redesigning market rules, and whether it brings benefits or not therefore depends on how

---

40   Steven J. K. Vogel, 'Why Freer Markets Need More Rules' in Naazneen H. Barma and Steven K. Vogel (eds), *The Political Economy Reader — Markets as Institutions*, Routledge, 2008.

well the market is analysed and how well the new rules are drawn up.

If we turn next to the transition of formerly planned economies to the market, as we saw in Chapter 1, the debate in Russia about how to move to a market economy was won by the radical privatisers. We also saw that their programme of rapid privatisation led to a collapse of the Russian economy, with industrial production falling by almost 60 per cent in the period 1990–99. And as it declined, the wealth of the country was divided up more inequitably. While in 1989 only 2 per cent of those living in Russia were in poverty, by late 1998 that number had risen to 23.8 per cent, using a \$2 a day standard.

In contrast, China adopted a strategy of gradually changing its institutions. As a result, while industrial production in Russia declined at an average annual rate of 5.6 per cent in the 1990s, China grew at an average rate of over 10 per cent. And while the Russian transition led to a vast increase in poverty, China's transition entailed the largest reduction in poverty in history in such a short time frame – from 358 million in 1990 to 208 million in 1997, using China's lower poverty standard of \$1 a day.

China's reforms began in agriculture, with the movement from the collective commune system of agricultural production to the 'individual responsibility' system – effectively partial privatisation. Individuals could not buy and sell land, but they could benefit from an increase in output. China also sought to eliminate the old economy by creating a new one. Millions of new enterprises sprang up, created by the townships and villages which no longer had to manage agricultural production. The Chinese government also invited foreign firms into the country to participate in joint ventures.

While the Russians failed to create the institutional infrastructure of a capitalist economy, the Chinese government gradually put one in place. This included an effective securities and exchange commission, bank regulations and safety nets. It also privatised much of the housing stock. And as safety nets were put in place and new jobs were created, it started to restructure the old state-owned enterprises. What happened in Russia and China demonstrates clearly the importance of building a regulatory structure and other key institutions of a functioning market economy before privatisation. Otherwise privatisation leads simply to wealth appropriation and to assets being taken abroad, as happened in Russia.

Finally, if we look at the economic performance of poor countries, neo-liberals argue that it is only necessary to get the prices right and everything else will fall into place. But advocates of Progressive capitalism argue that governments also need to develop the necessary economic institutions.

In many developing countries the state lacks both the people and the expertise to develop the necessary institutions for economic growth to take off. As a result, in order to win votes, politicians turn to the direct provision of goods and services, and other authoritarian approaches to allocating resources.

It can be seen from these three very different situations that the market-institutional perspective that underpins

Progressive capitalism has very important implications for politicians and policy-makers. It also raises very important questions in both developed and developing countries about whether politicians and policy-makers have the expertise and skills to reform markets that are not performing efficiently, as the expertise and resources needed to build and reform institutions are very different from those required simply to delete regulations.

In the first half of this book I have set out why we need a new Progressive political economy to guide us in the years ahead as we strive to improve our rate of economic growth and reduce financial instability and inequality. In this chapter I have also set out the basis of such a new Progressive political economy. In the second half of this book I will seek to show how this new Progressive political economy, when applied in practice, produces a very different set of policies to the failed ones that neo-liberals continue to advocate, and to show why these policies should be adopted if we want to create more prosperous and fairer economies.

FIVE

THE VARIETIES OF CAPITALISM

If there was a single universal best set of economic institutions, then the reform of a country's economic institutions would be a very simple matter. It would only be necessary to discover that best set of economic institutions and copy it. In recent years, however, a great deal of empirical research has been done on the institutions of economically successful countries, and this shows that there are at least two varieties of capitalism with very different institutions, and both perform equally well.[41] It also shows that mixing institutions from the two varieties of capitalism or trying to move from one variety of capitalism to another is not a recipe for success.

It is essential that politicians and policy-makers understand this research, as it will help them avoid some obvious

---

41 Peter A. Hall and David Soskice, 'An Introduction to Varieties of Capitalism', in Peter A. Hall and David Soskice (eds), *Varieties of Capitalism: The Institutional Foundations of Comparative Advantage*, Oxford University Press, 2001.

mistakes, and in this chapter I will describe this research and its implications. It is important research because in the period since the Second World War a succession of countries have been held up as models of capitalism which other countries should copy, though the reason why these countries are held up as models is usually nothing better than the fact that they are doing well economically at the time.

After the Second World War, France and Germany were first in the spotlight. Then it was argued that Japan had developed a superior version of capitalism, and I remember going to Japan in the 1980s and, like many other people, being totally convinced that the UK should adopt the Japanese model, not understanding that the Japanese had not discovered a superior form of capitalism or that transferring their economic institutions to a country like the UK would be impossible.

When the Japanese economy stalled at the start of the 1990s, the American model of capitalism, which seemed to be doing well at the time, was rediscovered and placed on a pinnacle. If the Chinese economy continues to grow as fast in the next ten years as it has done in recent years, books with titles such as *China as No. 1* will no doubt start to appear, urging other countries to copy the Chinese model, even though the reason China is growing so fast is that it is catching up with the countries who are pushing forward the world's technological frontier.

As a result of these claims, too often in the past politicians and policy-makers have tried unsuccessfully to import institutions from another variety of capitalism or switch over to it, when they could have been more usefully employed in analysing how well the economic institutions of their own country were working and seeking to improve their design.

While Andrew Shonfield in *Modern Capitalism*, his influential work of 1965, was the first person to draw attention to the different types of capitalism, the first person to try to classify these types was Michel Albert in his path-breaking book *Capitalisme contre Capitalisme*, published in 1991.[42] In his view, the hundred-year struggle between capitalism and collective state socialism, having been won by capitalism, had been replaced by a struggle between what he called the Rhine model of capitalism and the neo-American model. The Rhine model of capitalism covered not only the Rhine countries in the narrow geographical sense – Switzerland, Germany and the Netherlands – but also to some extent Scandinavia and, with allowances for the inevitable cultural differences, Japan as well.

The Rhine model, exemplified in Albert's view by Germany, emphasised collective success, consensus and long-term concerns, while the neo-American model was based on individual success and short-term gain. To Albert it was also obvious that the Rhine model was economically and socially superior, but to his dismay he saw it in retreat as countries were seduced by 'the siren song of the USA and the superficial

---

42 Michel Albert, *Capitalism Against Capitalism*, Whurr, 1993.

glitter of its casino economy'. If the Rhine model was to flourish, and the slide to the neo-American model to be halted, it would be through the political process of European integration.

Liberal Market Economies and Co-ordinated Market Economies

The German–USA dichotomy which Michel Albert put forward became, a decade later, the basis of the more theoretically based approach of Peter Hall and David Soskice. They identified two types of capitalist economy: liberal market economies (LMEs) and co-ordinated market economies (CMEs). The fundamental difference between these two types of capitalism lies in the way they achieve co-ordination.

In liberal market economies, firms co-ordinate their activities mainly using market relationships, and these market relationships take the form of the arm's-length exchange of goods and services in a context of competition and formal contracting. Markets generate price signals, and firms and individuals demand and supply goods and services in response.

In co-ordinated market economies, on the other hand, firms use market relationships extensively, but in addition they rely on non-market relationships to co-ordinate their actions with other actors in the economy and to create their core competences. These non-market relationships generally involve contracts with a greater element of trust, network monitoring based on the exchange of private information inside networks, and more use of collaborative as opposed to competitive relationships inside firms to build up their core competences. While market relationships are important to all firms, in co-ordinated market economies firms enter into more relationships which are not totally mediated by market forces.

It should also be noted that CMEs have two variants, one of which is found in Northern Europe and the other in Japan and Korea. In the Northern European variety, the basis of business co-ordination is the industrial sector, and we find unions, technology transfer, technical standard-setting, the training of engineers and the development of vocational training standards all taking place within an industry framework. These economies are, therefore, rightly described as 'industry-co-ordinated economies'.

In Japan and South Korea, on the other hand, the most intense co-ordination takes place within groups of companies, the vertical and horizontal *keiretsu* in Japan and the *chaebols* in Korea. In these economies we find unions, technology development and diffusion, technical standard-setting and vocational training all taking place on a group basis. These economies are, therefore, rightly described as 'group-co-ordinated economies'.

The next question has to be which countries come into each of our two varieties of capitalism. To some extent this has to be a matter of judgement but it is possible to provide some figures to inform such a judgement. A good starting point is to locate countries, as Peter Hall and David Soskice do, on two axes which measure them in terms of the scale of stock market capitalisation and the amount of employment protection. A large stock market indicates a greater reliance on markets to achieve co-ordination in the financial sphere, and high levels of employment protection tend to reflect higher levels of non-market co-ordination in the sphere of industrial relations.

Figure 5.1 Institutions Across Sub-spheres of the Political Economy

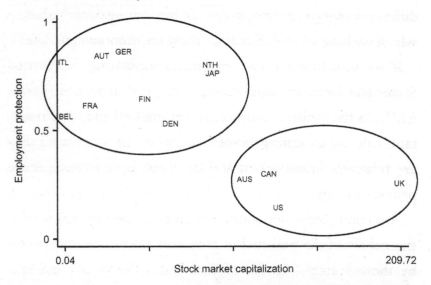

(Peter A. Hall and David Soskice, 'An Introduction to Varieties of Capitalism', in Peter A. Hall and David Soskice (ed.), *Varieties of Capitalism: The Institutional Foundations of Comparative Advantage*, Oxford University Press, 2001.)

As can be seen from Fig 5.1, if this is done for OECD countries, they form themselves into two groups, giving us a strong indication as to whether they are liberal market economies or co-ordinated market economies. On the basis of this analysis and other information, six large OECD countries (the USA, the UK, Australia, Canada, New Zealand and Ireland) should clearly be classified as liberal market economies, and another ten (Germany, Japan, Switzerland, the Netherlands, Belgium, Sweden, Norway, Denmark, Finland and Austria) should be classified as co-ordinated market economies.

The fundamental difference in the use of market and non-market relationships by liberal market economies and co-ordinated market economies means that we find important differences between them in each of the four institutional areas which we have identified as important for economic growth.

If we take first the case of financial markets, the United States and Germany can be seen as typical of an LME and a CME. In the United States, financial markets play an important role in allocating resources, while in Germany they are relatively unimportant and the banks have a much more prominent role.

A second dimension along which financial systems vary is the nature of the external control exercised over companies by those systems. In the United States the equity markets provide a market for corporate control, and hostile takeovers are used as a device for disciplining managers. In Germany, hostile takeovers are legally possible but do not occur much in practice, and it has been widely argued that monitoring by the *hausbank* system performs the same kind of external control as hostile takeovers in the USA.

In bank-based financial systems, companies have access to finance that is not totally dependent on publicly available financial data or current returns, and access to this kind of 'patient capital' makes it possible for them to retain a skilled workforce throughout economic downturns and to invest in projects which only generate returns in the long run. The difficulty here is that if finance is not to be dependent on balance-sheet criteria, investors must have other ways of monitoring the performance of companies in order to ensure that managers are enhancing the value of their investments, and this means that they need to have access to 'inside' information about the company.

In Germany this is achieved through dense networks which link the managers and technical personnel inside companies with their counterparties in other companies in a way which enables them to share reliable information about their companies. In Germany, for example, information about the operational performance of a company can be accessed by investors through a number of different routes. These include the close relationships that companies have with their clients and suppliers, the knowledge secured from extensive networks of cross-shareholdings, and the joint membership of capable industry associations that gather information about companies as a result of their work co-ordinating standard-setting, technology transfer and vocational training.

In contrast, countries such as the UK and USA which have very deep and varied financial markets don't usually have dense networks which are capable of providing investors with inside information, and consequently they have to rely more on quarterly financial results and publicly available information. This means that companies have to pay more attention to current earnings and the price of their shares on equity markets. As a result they are under more pressure to perform in the short-term, and this may result in them not making the long-term investments that they should do.

But while bank-based financial systems are better than market-based systems at providing 'patient capital' to firms in traditional sectors, they are less good at financing high-risk technological companies. Venture capital funds are difficult to develop in countries without large capital markets which support high-risk initial public offerings (IPOs), and financing 'gaps' for high-risk capital are usually found within them. They also usually lack experienced venture capitalists who can provide the young companies with the strategic advice and access to personal networks which are important for arranging key business alliances and recruiting key managers or scientists.

In the UK we have AIM, the London Stock Exchange market for smaller and growing companies, which was launched in 1995 and which has helped over 3,100 companies raise over £67 billion through new and further capital raisings. On the other hand, Germany's market for technology shares and other high-growth stocks, the Neuer Markt, which was launched in 1997, closed in 2002.

Turning now to corporate governance, we find in LMEs the 'shareholder' model of corporate governance, in which the maximisation of shareholder value is the primary goal of the company, while in CMEs we find the 'stakeholder' model, in which the interests of employees, suppliers and customers have to be balanced against each other.

In the first case the company is treated as a private association which needs some external regulation so that it acts in the public interest. In the second case the company is treated as a public body which has defined public purposes and responsibilities and which is 'constitutionalised' by a detailed specification of its internal governance structure.

The way that the two models work is expressed in different board systems and corporate institutions.[43] In the UK and the USA, which are prime examples of the 'shareholder' model, companies are generally run by a CEO-dominated single board. The board is elected by the shareholders and typically consists of a mix of outside directors and inside directors who are top executives of the company. The CEO is almost always on the board and usually plays a major role in choosing the other members of the board. As leader of the company, the CEO is expected to consult with other managers but then to make major decisions himself or herself and to take responsibility for them.

---

43   Franklin Allen and Douglas Gale, *Comparing Financial Systems*, MIT Press, 2001.

By contrast, in Germany, which is the prime example of the 'stakeholder' model, companies are characterised by a pluralist system. The clearest manifestation of this pluralist system is the dual board system that companies have. The supervisory board (*Aufsichtsrat*) is the controlling body, with half of its representatives elected by shareholders and half by employees. Strategic decisions such as major investments, mergers and acquisitions, dividend policy, changes in capital structures and the appointment of top managers is made by the board. The day-to-day running of the company, however, is the responsibility of the management board (*Vorstand*), which generally meets once a week and includes between five and ten top managers of the company. No one is allowed simultaneously to be a member of the supervisory and the management boards, and while the management board has a chair or speaker, a great deal of autonomy is given to the heads of functions such as finance, production, marketing and personnel. Major decisions on proposals to the supervisory board are usually reached through consensus.

A third important institutional area where LMEs and CMEs differ is in their training and educational systems. It is possible to distinguish three types of skills in industry: company-specific skills, industry-specific skills and general skills. These skills differ significantly in their transferability between companies. Company-specific skills are acquired through on-the-job training, and are least transferable. They are valuable to the company that carries out the training, but not to other employers. Industry-specific skills, particularly when they are properly certified, are valuable to any employer within a specific industry, and are acquired through apprenticeship and vocational schools. Finally, general skills are largely produced by the state educational system and have a value in all industries.

Company-specific skills are obviously not subject to poaching by companies and therefore successful companies in all countries are likely to provide training to their employees at an optimal level, but countries vary in their ability to produce industry-specific and general skills. This is clearly related to the institutions they have, and we can illustrate the nature of these differences by once again comparing Germany with the USA.

Germany excels in providing workers with industry-specific skills. This requires a considerable amount of co-ordination, as workers must be confident that training to be an apprentice, for example, will prepare them for a well-paid job, while companies investing in training need to know that it will give their workers useful skills, and that after they have trained them their workers will not be poached by companies that do not make equivalent investments in training.

This co-ordination is achieved in Germany by industry-wide employer associations and trade unions supervising a publicly subsidised training system. These bodies put pressure on major companies to take on apprentices and monitor their performance, and in this way they prevent companies free-riding on the training efforts of others. By negotiating industry-wide skill categories and training protocols in each industrial sector, they also ensure that the training fits companies' needs, and that there will be a demand for any apprentices not required by the companies at which they were apprenticed. And because German employer associations are strong and effective bodies who provide many benefits to their members, and to which most companies in a sector belong, they are able to provide the monitoring and persuasion that the operation of such a system demands. They are also able to provide the deliberative forums in which skill categories, training quotas and protocols can be negotiated.

In countries such as the USA, on the other hand, the education and training systems are generally associated with highly fluid labour markets. Whereas in countries which focus on industry-specific skills a selection process at an early stage pushes pupils along separate paths, a differentiation which makes sense where there are occupational and segmented labour markets, in countries such as the USA the education and training systems emphasise general education. This makes sense from the perspective of workers facing short job tenures and fluid labour markets as success depends on acquiring the general skills that can be used in many different companies.

In countries such as the USA, initial vocational training, to the extent it exists, is a 'low esteem' route. It is not seen as a good alternative to a university education but as something that is done by young people who have failed academically. It is also not seen to have much economic value.

At the same time, in such countries post-compulsory general education is usually strong, with large numbers of young people in higher education. Such countries also tend to have substantial doctoral programmes in basic sciences and engineering, but without close company linkages.

In each of the above three areas (financial markets, corporate governance, and education and training) we have seen major differences in the institutions which LMEs and CMEs have. These differences have been widely researched and are well understood. In the fourth institutional area which is important for economic growth, national systems of innovation, there are also important institutional differences between LMEs and CMEs, but these have not been researched as much and are not well understood. In the next section I will, therefore, set out what I perceive the differences to be, as they are very important when we come to look at the differences in economic performance of LMEs and CMEs.

National Systems of Innovation

While there have not been systematic comparisons of the national systems of innovation in LMEs and CMEs, it is possible to understand the differences between them by pulling together the relevant but fragmented work which has been done. A good starting point is an important paper produced by Henry Ergas for the Centre for European Studies entitled 'Does Technology Policy Matter?'[44] In this he distinguished between countries where technology policy was 'mission-oriented', in the sense of being primarily concerned with

---

44 Henry Ergas, 'Does Technology Policy Matter?', Centre for European Policy Studies Papers, No. 29, 1986.

major projects of national significance, and those countries where it was 'diffusion-oriented', in the sense of being largely concerned with upgrading the capacity of companies to respond to new technologies. The US, UK and France he put in the first category, and the Federal Republic of Germany, Switzerland and Sweden he put in the second category. Japanese technology policy he saw as having both mission-oriented and diffusion-oriented components.

In the mission-oriented countries, the primary goal of public policy, he argued, was the development of specific products or systems incorporating highly novel and sophisticated capabilities, while the diffusion-oriented countries were less concerned with developing new cutting-edge technologies and more concerned with diffusing widely technological capabilities throughout industry. In the latter case this was mainly done by industry itself, with trade associations playing a particularly important role in the Federal Republic of Germany and Switzerland.

In the same paper he distinguished between two types of adjustment to new opportunities: 'shifting', the transfer of resources from mature industries to emerging ones, and 'deepening', which involves increasing the productivity of resources in current industries. The United States, a paradigmatic case of 'shifting', he saw as specialising in the emergence phase of technological trajectories, while the Federal Republic of Germany, a paradigmatic case of 'deepening', he saw as specialising in the mature phases of technological trajectories.

Henry Ergas's paper is a useful starting point for looking at the different institutions which countries have for generating and transferring scientific and technological research. However, Henry Ergas was concerned only with technological research, whereas today, because of the closer connection we see between the development of emerging technologies and new scientific knowledge, we know that if we want to understand how research contributes to industrial competitiveness, we have to consider scientific research as well as technological research. Therefore, while I think it is useful to borrow his two categories, I think it is better to label them 'breakthrough-oriented' and 'diffusion-oriented'. 'Breakthrough-oriented' countries and 'diffusion-oriented' ones differ markedly in their institutions.

If we start by looking at the generation of scientific and technological research, we find considerable differences in the organisation and control of public science systems in different countries. To understand these differences it is necessary to recognise that in public science systems, the reputation of scientists, as judged by the publication of their research findings in prestigious scientific journals, is of critical importance.[45] The differences between public science systems can then be analysed in terms of two key characteristics: the intensity of reputational competition between researchers and the extent of intellectual pluralism and flexibility.

---

45   Richard Whitley, 'Competition and Pluralism in the public sciences: the impact of institutional frameworks on the organisation of academic science', *Research Policy* 32 (2003).

'Breakthrough-oriented' countries are those which have a high level of reputational competition and of pluralism and flexibility, while 'diffusion-oriented' countries are ones which have a low level.

In a country such as the USA, reputational competition is strong and this results in new ideas, findings and approaches being quickly communicated to other researchers as scientists seek to build their reputations. In a country such as Japan, however, where researchers are more dependent on research institutes or similar employers than on their reputation with their specialist colleagues, reputational competition is lower and the rate of new knowledge production less.

Secondly, the levels of intellectual pluralism, and flexibility in changing research goals, vary in different public science systems. Where pluralism and flexibility are high, scientists are able to pursue a wide variety of intellectual projects with distinctive goals and approaches, and to change direction quickly. As a result they are more likely to do research that both seeks to understand fundamental physical and biological processes and to deal with technologically oriented issues. Additionally, new fields focused on technological concerns can become institutionalised more easily as legitimate areas of research.

While 'breakthrough-oriented' countries, which have high levels of reputational competition, pluralism and flexibility, will be more likely to produce radical innovation, they are less likely to produce the incremental innovation which arises from long-term research programmes focused on the specific opportunities and problems of particular industries. This is more likely to be produced in 'diffusion-oriented' countries, with their low level of reputational competition and low level of pluralism and flexibility.

It might be thought from the above discussion, and from the political debate in the USA in the last thirty years, that a 'breakthrough-oriented' country like the United States only supports scientific and technological research through funding bodies such as the National Science Foundation (NSF) and the National Institute of Health (NIH), which allocate funds to basic science through the peer-review process. But the reality is very different, and over this period the federal government has dramatically increased its targeted resourcing of scientific and technological research in order to advance new technologies in the business economy. Political ideology, however, has made these efforts largely invisible to mainstream public debate.[46]

Targeted resourcing in this context means government officials identifying important technological challenges, the solution of which would open up important commercial opportunities to industry, and then providing funding to groups that have promising ideas for achieving breakthroughs in these areas. A key body in this funding has been an office in the Pentagon, the Advanced Research Projects Agency (ARPA), which established a new model for technology policy. This involved hiring a small number of visionary

---

46   Fred Block, 'Swimming Against the Current: The Rise of a Hidden Development State in the United States', Special issue of *Politics and Society*, Vol. 36, No. 2, 2008.

technologists and giving them a high degree of autonomy to give out research funds. These technologists are proactive rather than reactive and aim to set an agenda for researchers in each field.

Three examples of targeted resourcing by the US government are worth mentioning. ARPA's Information Processing Techniques Office was set up in 1962 and played a central role in the advance of computer technology in the 1960s and 1970s. The internet itself began as an ARPA project in the 1960s to improve communication among computer researchers funded by the agency, while many of the technologies that were ultimately incorporated into the personal computer were developed by ARPA-funded researchers.

A second important initiative of ARPA was the creation of Sematech in 1987 as a result of pressure from the US semiconductor industry for a response to strong Japanese competition. Sematech was a consortium of twelve semiconductor firms, initially financed with $100 million per year of ARPA money and contributions from the consortium members. Its mission was to upgrade technological capacity all along the semiconductor manufacturing value chain, and to create an ongoing research and education infrastructure 'for sustained US leadership in semiconductor technology'. In this aim it was largely successful, enabling the US semiconductor industry to regain significant market share from foreign competitors, and after ten years it became self-supporting.

The third initiative worth mentioning was the support given to the emergence of genetic engineering by the NIH.

The NIH did not set technological goals the way ARPA did, and it relied heavily on the peer-review model for funding research. However, its funding mandate relied heavily on fighting human disease, and once NIH officials grasped the disease-fighting possibilities of genetic engineering, they put huge resources into advancing the technology. The result was a vast increase in the late 1980s in genetic engineering research projects, followed by a rapid growth in biotechnology firms.

A mention also ought to be made of the Small Business Innovation Research programme, under which all government agencies that fund a significant amount of R&D are required to reserve 2.5 per cent of their research budgets to fund initiatives by small businesses. The agencies specify the areas where they would like to see innovation, and award grants competitively in them. The grants do not have to be repaid, and the small businesses retain full control of the resulting intellectual property. Total funding under this programme was $2 billion in 2004.

It will be argued, of course, that these and other initiatives of the US government, even if they are successful, are too small to be significant as far as the innovation performance of the USA economy is concerned. But there is evidence that this is not the case.

For the last forty-five years, R&D magazine has been listing the 100 most innovative commercial products introduced in the previous year. In 2006, fifty out of eighty-eight domestic innovations were the products of researchers at US government laboratories, universities or other public agencies, another thirteen came from spin-offs that had received considerable federal funding, and of the remaining twenty-five innovations produced by private sector organisations, at least another fourteen involved federal dollars. These figures suggest very strongly that government funding of scientific and technological research has a major impact on the US innovation performance.

Turning now to the second key dimension of national systems of innovation we also find considerable differences in the university–industry interactions in different countries, and these can be illustrated by comparing again the USA, the paradigmatic example of a 'breakthrough-oriented' country with Germany, the paradigmatic example of a 'diffusion-oriented' one. In Germany, various institutions such as the An-Institutes and the Fraunhofer Institutions support short-term problem-solving in universities, while in the United States, University-Industry Research Centres (UIRCS) are used to fund five-year research programmes which will be useful to industry.[47]

In the last three decades, spin-out companies from universities have also been a very useful institution to transform research breakthroughs into marketable products, and it is an area where the USA has led the way. By comparison, German universities have had a low number of spin-outs. There are many reasons for the large number of spin-outs in the USA: the availability of venture capital, the large scale of

---

47 Ulrich Schmoch, 'Interaction of Universities and Industrial Enterprises in Germany and the United States – A Comparison', *Industry and Innovation*, Vol. 6, No. 1, June 1999.

the domestic market, the bankruptcy law and sophisticated financial markets for IPOs, but of critical importance is the different way that universities are administered in the USA as compared with Germany. In the USA, universities, both public and private, are administered in a very entrepreneurial way, and can take a share in their spin-outs, and in that way profit from their economic success. In Germany, by contrast, universities have a public, non-profit status, are administered according to public regulations and can only provide conditions which support spin-outs.

The part played in the transformation of research breakthroughs into marketable products by American universities has been both inspired and legitimised by the concept of the 'entrepreneurial university'.[48] Originally conceived as institutions of cultural conservation and transmission, universities in the late nineteenth and early twentieth centuries, starting in Germany, experienced an academic revolution, as a result of which research became an accepted task. Then, starting at MIT just before the Second World War, universities in the USA began to take on a third role, that of transferring knowledge into industry, and the 'entrepreneurial university' was born. This model of the university has now been widely adopted in the USA and has spread to the UK.

The 'entrepreneurial university' builds partly on the development of the scientific research capabilities which grew as a result of the first academic revolution, and partly on the creation

---

48   Henry Etzkowitz, *MIT and the Rise of Entrepreneurial Science*, Routledge, 2002.

of a series of boundary-spanning mechanisms, including technology transfer offices, spin-off companies, incubator facilities and science parks. The fact that academics are used to being more entrepreneurial in their competition for funds in countries like the USA and the UK means that this concept has spread faster in these countries than in countries where the professor is a civil servant.

The Performance of LMEs and CMEs

We have seen that LMEs and CMEs have very different institutions in areas which are of key importance for economic growth: financial markets, corporate governance, education and training systems and national systems of innovation. This raises two very interesting questions for politicians and policy-makers. Firstly, does one or other of the varieties of capitalism perform economically better than the other over long periods of time and, secondly, do the two varieties of capitalism support different kinds of competitive advantage which make it likely that the firms of a particular country will do better in some industries and industry segments than others?

The answer to the first question is that neither variety of capitalism is consistently better than the other, and the task of economic policy-makers has therefore to be the improvement of their particular variety of capitalism and its constant adaptation to the changing economic and technological opportunities and challenges that it faces. If we look at the major indicators of economic performance displayed in Table 5.1, we can see that there is no systematic difference between the two varieties of capitalism in terms of the rate of economic growth. It is therefore wrong to see the existence of different varieties of capitalism as leading inevitably to a 'battle of systems'.

Table 5.1 The Economic Performance of LMEs and CMEs

Liberal market economies

	Growth rate of GDP			GDP per capita		Unemployment rate		
	61–73	74–84	85–98	74–84	85–97	60–73	74–84	85–98
Australia	5.2	2.8	3.3	7932	16701	1.9	6.2	8.5
Canada	5.3	3.0	2.3	9160	18835	5.1	8.4	9.5
Ireland	4.4	3.9	6.5	4751	12830	5.0	9.1	14.1
New Zealand	4.0	1.8	1.7	7378	14172	0.2	2.2	6.9
UK	3.1	1.3	2.4	7359	15942	2.0	6.7	8.7
United States	4.0	2.2	2.9	11055	22862	4.9	7.5	6.0
LME average	4.3	2.5	3.2	7939	16890	3.2	6.7	8.9

Coordinated market economies

	Growth rate of GDP			GDP per capita		Unemployment rate		
	61–73	74–84	85–98	74–84	85–97	60–73	74–84	85–98
Austria[a]	4.9	2.3	2.5	7852	17414	1.6	2.2	5.3
Belgium	4.9	2.0	2.2	8007	17576	2.2	8.2	11.3
Denmark	4.4	1.8	2.2	8354	18618	1.4	7.1	9.3
Finland	5.0	2.7	2.2	7219	15619	2.0	4.8	9.4
Iceland	5.7	4.1	2.7	8319	18285	0.6	0.6	2.5
Germany	4.3	1.8	2.2	7542	16933	0.8	4.6	8.5
Japan	9.7	3.3	2.6	7437	18475	1.3	2.1	2.8
Netherlands[b]	4.9	1.9	2.8	7872	16579	1.5	5.6	6.8
Norway	4.3	4.0	2.9	8181	19325	1.6	2.1	4.3
Sweden	4.2	1.8	1.5	8450	16710	1.9	2.3	4.8
Switzerland	4.4	.58	1.3	10680	21398	.01	0.4	2.5
CME average	5.1	2.4	2.3	8174	17902	1.3	3.6	6.1

(Peter A. Hall and David Soskice, op cit. *Varieties of Capitalism: The Institutional Foundations of Comparative Advantage*, Oxford University Press, 2001.)

In answer to the second question, however, the different institutions of liberal market economies and co-ordinated market economies appear very clearly to provide firms with advantages in performing different types of activities, and this in turn enables them to produce some kinds of goods and services more efficiently than others.

The main way that liberal market economies and co-ordinated market economies differ in the support that they give to firms to build competitive advantage lies in the different support that they give to innovation. Liberal market economies are very effective at supporting radical innovation which involves major new product designs, the development of totally new goods or major changes to production processes, while co-ordinated market economies give greater support to incremental innovation, small-scale but continuous improvements to existing product lines and production processes.

This fact helps to explain why countries excel in different industry sectors, because radical innovation is important in some industries while incremental innovation is important in others. Radical innovation is important, for example, in industries such as biotechnology, semiconductors and software development, which depend for success on research and rapid product development. It is also important in industries where success involves the supply of complex system-based products such as telecommunication and defence systems, and in service industries such as airlines, corporate finance, entertainment and advertising, which involve high-risk new product strategies and the rapid implementation of such strategies within large, tightly coupled organisations that employ a wide variety of people.

Incremental innovation, on the other hand, is important in

capital goods industries such as handling equipment and machine tools, consumer durables, engines and specialised transport equipment, where competitive success depends on being able to maintain high levels of quality while introducing incremental improvements to attract customer loyalty and hold down costs.

Two major data sets, compiled by Hall and Soskice, support this view of comparative institutional advantage. The first, using data from the European Patent Office, measures the

Fig 5.2 Patent Specialisation by Technology Classes in the United States, 1983–84 and 1993–94

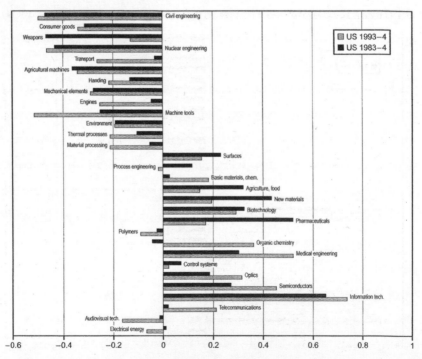

(Peter A. Hall and David Soskice, 'An Introduction to Varieties of Capitalism' in Peter A. Hall and David Soskice (eds), *Varieties of Capitalism: The Institutional Foundations of Comparative Advantage*, Oxford University Press, 2001.)

degree to which innovation in Germany and the United States is found in each of thirty technology classes, which vary in the extent to which technological progress in them is radical or incremental. Fig 5.2 charts the patent specialisation by technology classes in the United States, and Fig 5.3 the patent specialisation by technology classes in the Federal Republic of Germany. In each case the charts include data from 1993 to 1994 as well as from 1983 to 1984 in order to see whether the pattern is stable over time.

Fig 5.3 Patent Specialisation by Technology Classes in the Federal Republic of Germany, 1983–84 and 1993–94

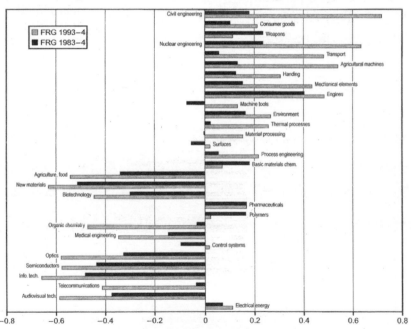

(Peter A. Hall and David Soskice, 'An Introduction to Varieties of Capitalism' in Peter A. Hall and David Soskice (eds), *Varieties of Capitalism: The Institutional Foundations of Comparative Advantage*, Oxford University Press, 2001.)

The striking findings are that Germany specialises in technological developments which are the reverse of those in which the USA specialises, that the pattern is consistent over time, and that it is exactly the pattern that the varieties of capitalism theory would predict. Firms in Germany have specialised in fields which are characterised by incremental innovation, including mechanical engineering, product handling, transport, consumer durables and machine tools, while firms in the United States specialise in fields where radical innovation is important, such as medical engineering, biotechnology, semiconductors and telecommunications.

The second data set is one based on work done by Michael Porter for his book *The Competitive Advantage of Nations*. This provides a large amount of relevant information about the economies of Germany, Sweden and Switzerland, which are examples of industry co-ordinated economies, and for the United States and the United Kingdom, which are examples of liberal market economies. Using the SITC trade classification of industries, Porter lists for each of his economies the industries in 1985 with a larger export share than the country's aggregate export share, and divides them up into four groups: primary goods, machinery, speciality inputs and services. On the basis of this data, David Soskice[49] calculated

---

49 David Soskice, 'Divergent Production Regimes: Co-ordinated and Unco-ordinated Market Economies in the 1980s, and 1990s', in Herbert Kitschelt, Peter Lange, Gerry Marks, John D. Stephens (eds), *Continuity and Change in Contemporary Capitalism*, Cambridge University Press, 1999.

that the number of 'internationally competitive' industries in each country was:

Germany 46
Switzerland 35
Sweden 28
United Kingdom 18
United States 17

However, the picture for internationally competitive services was almost exactly the reverse:

Germany 7
Sweden 9
Switzerland 14
United Kingdom 27
United States 44

These figures need to be treated with some caution as there were some classification problems with the UK data, but nevertheless they support the view that the co-ordinated market economies tend to produce complex products, which involve complex production processes and depend on skilled and experienced employees on whom responsibility can be devolved. Equally, they seem to show that liberal market economies tend to do better in services which involve the individual skills of highly trained and mobile professionals, and in the management of large, complex, tightly coupled systems such as airlines and telecommunications systems which require top management to be able to impose rapid changes through large organisations.

Finally, Peter Hall and David Soskice argue that as well as explaining the patterns of international trade, comparative institutional advantage also explains what they call institutional arbitrage. This is what happens when companies locate particular activities in other countries in order to obtain the advantages that the institutions of these countries can provide. This is the reason, they claim, why German pharmaceutical firms, located in a co-ordinated market economy, open research laboratories in the United States in order to access institutional support for radical innovation, and why a company like General Motors, located in a liberal market economy, builds an engine plant in Düsseldorf in order to gain access to the quality control, skill levels and capacities that German institutions foster.

Economic Reform and Varieties of Capitalism

The economic literature on the 'varieties of capitalism' should be of great interest to politicians and policy-makers, because it strongly supports a major theme of this book, which is that the economic performance of a country depends to a very considerable extent on its economic institutions. The 'variety of capitalism' literature also has two important lessons for politicians and policy-makers.

The first of these is that policy-makers should be very careful about trying to cherry-pick the economic institutions of a different variety of capitalism. At first sight it may seem very sensible, for example, for an LME to copy the technician training system of a co-ordinated market economy such as Germany, given the high quality and high reputation of the German one.

But there is a good reason for not trying to do so. The reason why the different institutional forms of capitalism are not scattered randomly across countries, and why some countries have more market-based institutions and others have more non-market-based institutions, lies in the complementarities which exist between different types of institutions. In economics, two goods are said to be complementary when increasing the amount of one good raises the marginal contribution of the other, and two institutions can be said to be complementary when the presence of one increases the efficiency of the other.

In the case of technician education in Germany, as we have seen, this depends to a considerable extent on co-ordination across firms in an industry, which in Germany is achieved by industry associations and trade unions supervising a publicly subsidised training system. This system cannot be transferred easily to the UK because we do not have strong industry associations and trade unions who could deliver such a training system. This may seem an obvious point, but for over a century the UK has looked admiringly at the German system, occasionally making half-hearted attempts to copy it, apparently without ever realising that this was a strategy doomed to failure.

While countries should not seek to cherry-pick the institutions of countries which have a different variety of capitalism, they should not hesitate to look at the institutions of other countries that have a similar variety of capitalism and, when those countries perform better, to copy them. For example, as we shall see in the next chapter, the UK has in recent years successfully copied a number of important institutional ideas from the USA in the field of innovation policy, and we should go on looking for additional ones.

The second lesson which politicians and policy-makers should learn from the 'varieties of capitalism' literature is that it is very difficult to switch to a different variety of capitalism. As we have seen, it is not obviously the case that one variety of capitalism consistently performs better than another. But this has not stopped endless books being written urging countries to copy the Japanese, German or American variety. A great deal of time has also been spent debating whether a country should model itself on another country or not, and in a few cases countries have actually attempted to do so.

The attempts by some countries to switch to another variety of capitalism have, however, demonstrated that it is an extremely difficult thing to do unless there is huge political commitment. The most explicit attempt to switch to another variety – that of French governments to create a German-style CME in France between the mid-1980s and the mid-1990s – was a total failure. While the Chirac administration of 1986 to 1988 identified explicitly with the ideas of Reagan and Thatcher, it was not prepared simply to entrust French industry to market forces. This is not altogether surprising as the right had administered the *dirigiste* state apparatus without interruption from 1958 to 1981. The Chirac administration privatised thirteen large groups, but instead of auctioneering the companies to the highest bidder, it sought to structure French capitalism along German or Japanese lines. Foreigners were barred from acquiring more than a 20 per cent stake in the privatised companies, and the government allocated a controlling stake in each company to a select group of investors, creating *noyaux durs*, or hardcore owners. These companies held each other's shares, and it was envisaged that in this way they would provide mutual takeover protection and patient capital.

The main supporters of the idea of transforming France into a CME like Germany (though they did not use that term) were France's so-called 'Second Left' or 'New Left' which emerged in the late 1960s and 1970s under Michel Rocard.[50] In the three years he was Prime Minister between 1988 and 1991, Rocard promoted decentralisation as a means of servicing the needs of small and medium-sized enterprises; endorsed the Auroux laws of 1982 as a necessary set of arrangements for introducing flexibility into production operations and tapping the latent productivity within each worker; and elevated the system of *noyaux durs* and equity cross-holdings into an economic strategy.

The Auroux laws of 1982 were designed to give workers new rights in the workplace. Workers would gain the right

---

50   Jonah D. Levy, *Tocqueville's Revenge*, Harvard University Press, 1999.

of free speech through the institution of 'expression groups' in companies with over 200 employees, as well as the right to participate in, and have control over, a range of key work-force issues as a result of legislation requiring branch-level or firm-level bargaining. At the same time employers would be required to consult with plant-level works councils on a range of issues such as the organisation of production, working hours, hiring and firing, working conditions, introduction of new technologies and major financial decisions.

In the mid-1980s, French officials were also converted to the *banque-industrie* model, a partnership between finance and industry similar to that in Germany, and in the late 1980s the government actively encouraged France's largest banks and insurance companies to copy the practices of the top German banks by taking equity stakes in leading firms, particularly public sector enterprises.

These policies had the great advantage of allowing the left to counter the right's enthusiasm for Reagan and Thatcher with the success of Modell Deutschland. In addition, Germany's social market economy offered a more reassuring social vision than American style '*liberalisme sauvage*'. It offered a way of removing the heavy hand of the state without opening the door to American inequalities and social pathologies.

But whereas in Germany a well-established network of societal and local organisations shouldered critical economic responsibilities, in France economic powers were concentrated in the *dirigiste* state. To forge a CME-style economy would have entailed not only changing a set of policies but also the actors as well, and this proved impossible to do, with the result that by the year 2000 the French economy looked very like a liberal market economy.

If we look first at the industrial relations field, we find that the policy lacked the strength to impose collective agreements in the place of state edicts. Before 1985 public officials were the dominant players in a field of weak employers' associations and even weaker unions, a fact which was reflected in three features of the industrial relations system. Firstly, the state was a significant employer, and its negotiations with its employees influenced private sector negotiations. Secondly, the minimum wage after 1970 increasingly became an important tool for policy-makers. Thirdly, the extension procedure, which allowed the government to extend agreements reached with one union to workers in an entire sector, was a powerful policy tool of the state. By 1985 the proportion of the workforce covered by such agreements had reached 94 per cent.

While these policies often aimed to facilitate the role of unions in collective bargaining, their overall effect was to divorce the level of wages from the negotiating and organisational capabilities of unions and employers. As Pepper D. Culpepper has written, 'The statist system of industrial relations thus promoted the development of social organisations whose strength lay in the law, the street, or the legislature, but not in firms themselves.'[51]

---

51 Pepper D. Culpepper 'Capitalism, Co-ordination and Economic Change: the French Political Economy since 1985' in Pepper D. Culpepper, Peter A. Hall and Bruno Palier (eds), *Changing France – The Politics that Markets Make*, Palgrave Macmillan, 2008.

The withdrawal of the state as a result led not to German-style institutions but to employer-driven deregulation.

The *banque-industrie* model also failed for institutional reasons. Post-war *dirigiste* policy-making had not prepared France's banks for the *banque-industrie* mission, and economic liberalisation squeezed the banks as both lenders and borrowers. The institutional underpinning of the *banque-industrie* project was also not very successful and finally collapsed between 1997 and 1999 as members of the *noyaux durs* sold off holdings in order to restore their balance sheets and refocus on their core missions.

While there continues to be an abiding belief in France that social negotiations rather than market forces are at the heart of the French economy, France has clearly ceased to have the statist political economy which it had during the so-called *trente glorieuses*, the thirty glorious years of post-war expansion. At the same time a German-style CME has not emerged in spite of efforts to create one, due to France's lack of strong employers' associations and trade unions, and its weak banks, and today it is difficult to see it as anything other than an LME.

The implication of the 'variety of capitalism' literature for politicians and policy-makers is clear. They should not try to change the variety of capitalism that their country has inherited or seek to import specific institutions from a different variety of capitalism. Instead they should decide what function they want each institution in their economy to perform, and then seek to make changes to them so that they perform better, borrowing ideas where available from a similar variety of capitalism.

This is not an easy task, requiring politicians and policy-makers to have a knowledge of how institutions work in practice at home and abroad, but it is essential if the economic growth of a country is to be improved, and in the next two chapters we will look at how such institutional improvements can best be made.

SIX

A PROGRAMME OF
FINANCIAL REFORM

As well as having a new Progressive political economy, based on an understanding of the processes of economic growth and which reflects Progressive beliefs, Progressive policy-makers need to have the knowledge and analytical skills to turn it into practical policies which respond to their country's current opportunities and problems. If the aim is to produce policies which improve the productivity and innovation of firms and makes them better able to compete in global markets, Progressive policy-makers need to stop putting forward simplistic solutions such as copying the institutions of whichever country is doing best at the time or mindlessly having the state take over any economic institution which appears to be functioning badly.

They need instead to have the capability to analyse how efficiently their country's economic institutions are functioning, and then to develop and implement policies to improve them.

They should also start talking about having a programme of economic reform rather than having an industrial policy, which is a term that has lost all meaning but which in most people's minds is associated with government in some way trying to control the corporate strategies of firms. Progressive policy-makers should be clear that their aim is solely to produce the conditions which best enable firms to innovate and grow profitably, and that it is the job of the directors of firms to determine their strategies.

To illustrate what politicians and policy-makers need to do, and how the ideas and values of Progressive capitalism can be turned into practical policies, I will look in this chapter at the changes that have taken place in equity markets in the UK in the last fifty years, what impact this has had on the 'pre-distribution of wealth' and the governance of companies, and what reforms government needs to make to the underlying institutions in order to make them function more effectively.

In the next chapter I will look at the infrastructure of the knowledge economy in the UK that companies need in order to create competitive advantage, namely our national system of innovation and our system of education and training, and at the ways those systems need to be reformed so that the rate of economic growth of the country improves. I have chosen in both cases to look mainly at the situation in the UK because I think it is fairly typical of the challenges that face developed countries in this policy space, and because it is the country whose institutions I know best.

The Reform of the UK's Equity Markets

The process of improving the design of an institution basically involves asking two questions. The first question is, what function do we want the institution we are analysing to perform, and is it performing it efficiently, and the second question is, can we design an institution which will perform the function better. In almost all cases the design of a more efficient institution will involve better aligning the incentives of the people who work in the institution with its function, or making certain that they have better sources of information.

What, then, is the purpose of UK equity markets? The long-term purpose of financial markets is to allocate capital to high-performing companies, and in that way provide savers with high returns, and to do so on the basis of low transaction costs. It is, however, important to understand that UK equity markets are no longer a significant source of funding for new investment by UK companies. Large UK companies are self-financing, the cash flow generated by their operations being more than they need for investment, and the relatively small number of UK companies which access the new issue market often use it as a means of achieving liquidity for early-stage investors, rather than to raise funds for new investment.

In this context, competition between asset managers on the basis of relative performance is inherently a zero-sum game. The asset management industry can benefit its customers — that is, its savers taken as a whole — only to the extent that its activities improve the performance of investee companies.

155

There is thus a conflict between the imperatives of the business model of asset managers, and the interests of UK businesses and those who invest in them, and this can lead to the appropriation of wealth by asset managers, as has happened in recent years.

The principal goals of UK equity markets should be to sustain and improve high-performing companies, and to earn good returns for savers without undue risk. The two goals in the long run are essentially the same, as the profits earned by high-performing companies are the only source of returns for savers who invest in equities.

There is also now a fairly general belief that UK financial markets have not performed well in terms of promoting good governance and stewardship and delivering good returns to savers as a result. The returns received by savers over recent years have been low and transaction costs have been enormous, with the financial sector taking for itself some 40 per cent of all corporate profits in the years before the 2008 financial crash, and bankers paying themselves huge bonuses.

The annual inflation-adjusted return on UK pension funds between 1963 and 1999 was 5.0 per cent, but averaged only around 1.1 per cent between 2000 and 2009.[52] This poor financial performance has contributed significantly to the massive deficits which pension funds have suffered, which

---

52   IFSL Research Pension Markets, 2010.

in turn has led to sponsoring companies having to transfer additional funds to them, as well as to reductions to benefits and scheme closures.

The returns to pension funds are after the fees that they are charged. These in total can vary between 0.5 per cent and 3 per cent, and have a significant impact on the final value of a pension. For example, if the fees are 2 per cent rather than 1 per cent, this will reduce the final value of the pension by about 20 per cent. It is, however, very difficult to establish what is the total level of fees a pension fund is being charged, and this lack of information means that the market does not work well. There is an urgent need, therefore, for a standard way of calculating and reporting the fees that a pension fund is charged.

In 1940 Fred Schwed, a stockbroker, published a famous book on how the stock market really works.[53] The title of his book, *Where are the Customers' Yachts?* is taken from an old Wall Street joke: a tourist is being shown all the beautiful boats in the harbour, and is told that some belong to bankers and some to stockbrokers, and when he asks innocently 'Where are the customers' yachts?', he is told there aren't any. A similar story could be told about London's equity markets and the pay of bankers in recent years.

The share of net income received by the top 1 per cent in

---

53 Fred Schwed Jr., *Where are the Customers' Yachts?: Or a Good Hard Look at Wall Street*, Wiley, 1990/1995.

the UK shrank from 12.6 per cent in 1937 to 4.2 per cent in 1978. It then started rising, and was back to 10 per cent by 2000, a great deal closer to the level last seen in the 1930s. The share of an even smaller group – the top 0.5 per cent – followed a very similar path. And the biggest cause of the rise in income inequality in the UK in recent years has been the pay explosion in the City. In the decade to 2008, three-quarters of the increase in income concentration among the top 1 per cent went to finance workers, mostly in the form of bonuses.[54]

The view that financial markets have not performed their function well is also widely held. In their evidence to the 'Kay Review of UK Equity Markets and Long-Term Decision Making', the Association of Chartered Certified Accountants (ACCA) observed that,

> it is sometimes forgotten that equity markets exist not solely to enrich speculators, market makers and intermediaries ... It would seem fair to say that equity markets today serve the needs of the players in these markets better than they serve either those who put up the money or the businesses wanting finance to support growth.

In their evidence to the same review, the Association of British Insurers (ABI) observed that 'regulation and market practice designed to ensure important but secondary goals

---

54   Stewart Lansley, *The Cost of Inequality*, Gibson Square, 2012.

may be obstructing the primary purpose', while the Financial Services Consumer Panel (FSCP) told the Review that 'aggregate capital values have not advanced over the past fifteen years, a period through which, until recently, the economy was growing steadily and when the financial sector was doing particularly well'.[55]

How has this situation come about? A major reason is the increased fragmentation of the shareholdings of UK equities. Fifty years ago, most shares in the UK were held by individuals who were advised by stockbrokers who had direct knowledge of both their clients and the companies in which they invested. By the 1990s, this structure had changed and UK equities were largely owned by UK financial institutions, primarily insurance companies and pension funds. In the last two decades, however, this structure has changed once again, as there has been a significant rise in the scale of foreign ownership, a consequence of the globalisation of both corporate activities and equity investment strategies. Individual shareholders excluding holdings in nominee accounts are 11 per cent (including them, the figure is thought to be closer to 20 per cent). The holdings of pension funds and insurance companies now account for around 14 per cent of the total, and the share attributed to non-UK holders is over 40 per cent. This fragmentation has reduced the incentives for engagement and the level of control enjoyed by each shareholder.

---

55 Interim Report of the Kay Review of UK Equity Markets and Long-Term Decision Making.

Table 6.1 Historical Trends in Beneficial Ownership (percentage held)

	1963	1975	1981	1991	2001	2008	2010
Rest of the world	7	5.6	3.6	12.8	35.7	41.5	41.2
Insurance companies	10	15.9	20.5	20.8	20	13.4	8.6
Pension funds	6.4	16.8	26.7	31.3	16.1	12.8	5.1
Individuals	54	37.5	28.2	19.9	14.8	10.2	11.5
Other	22.6	24.2	21	15.2	13.4	22.1	33.6

('Final Report of the Kay Review of UK Equity Markets and Long-Term Decision-Making'.)

At the same time there has been a massive growth in the amount of intermediation in equity investment, driven both by a desire for greater professionalism and efficiency, and by a decline in trust and confidence in the investment chain. Between the saver and the company we now find trustees, investment consultants, managers who allocate funds to specialist asset managers, agents who 'wrap' products, and investment managers who have become the key agent in the investment chain.

The growth of intermediation has led to increased costs for investors, and an increased potential for misaligned incentives. The financial targets of the business model of the investment manager are not necessarily identical with the interests of either the companies which use equity markets or the savers who provide funds to them. The growth of intermediation has also led to a tendency to see the performance of the market through the eyes of intermediaries. Goals such as liquidity, transparency and price discovery have come to be regarded as ends in themselves, and not as intermediate steps towards the goals of high performing companies and good returns for savers.

These changes in financial markets have led to two major principal–agent problems, the first between the savers and investment managers and the second between the investment managers and the companies in which they invest. The principal–agent problem in the case of the relationship between the savers and the investment managers has been clearly described by Paul Woolley of the London School of Economics.[56] In his description of the situation, the principals are the providers of capital who subcontract financial tasks to agents, who are often professional investment managers. This delegation leads to asymmetric information (the agents have more and better information than their principals) and a major incentive problem because the interests of the two groups are rarely the same.

The principal–agent problem can be used to explain some key features of modern financial markets such as momentum, the commonly observed tendency for price changes of shares to overshoot, which in extreme form produces bubbles and crashes. The existence of momentum has been

---

56 Paul Woolley, 'Why are Financial Markets So Inefficient and Exploitative – And a Suggested Remedy', in *The Future of Finance – the LSE Report*, The London School of Economics and Political Science, 2010.

extensively documented in empirical studies of securities but has proved difficult to explain if one believes the efficient market theory.

The reason the asymmetric information of agents and principals leads to momentum is that investors have imperfect knowledge of the ability of investment managers they invest in. They don't know whether underperformance against a benchmark arises from the investment manager's prudent avoidance of over-priced stocks or is a sign of incompetence. If the shortfall grows, however, investors are likely to conclude that the reason is incompetence, and as a result transfer funds to an outperforming manager, thereby amplifying the price changes that led to the initial underperformance and generating momentum. If asset prices are formed in this way, it would also provide an explanation of how short-term incentives such as annual performance fees cause fund managers to concentrate on high-turnover trend-following strategies that add to the distortion in markets.

The high turnover which arises from momentum trading comes at a heavy cost to long-term investors and leads to significant wealth appropriation by agents. Active management and its associated trading costs based on 100 per cent annual turnover, which is a reasonable assumption, erode the value of a pension fund by around 1 per cent per annum. The assets of pension funds are being exchanged with other pension funds twenty-five times during the life of the average liability for no collective advantage but at a cost that reduces the end-value of the pension by up to 25 per cent.

The dysfunctionality of today's equity markets is made even worse in periods of financial innovation as it becomes harder for the outsider to understand everything that insiders are doing and difficult to monitor their actions. Financial innovation also increases the problem of moral hazard, that is, the risk that fund managers (in this case) will pursue their own interests rather than those of their clients either because they have limited liability in the legal sense or because their fees enable them to participate in gains but do not require them to suffer losses. This encourages them to invest their clients' money in high-risk ventures. The past decade has seen a very significant increase in new products, as strategies such as hedge funds, securitisation, private equity, structured finance, CDOs and credit default swaps have multiplied. Each of these innovations was approved on the basis that they 'complete' markets and spread risk-bearing by offering investors and borrowers new ways of packaging risk and return. But the end result of all this activity was huge bonuses for the bankers and low returns for investors.

This misalignment of the interests of the savers and the investment managers was made worse by the latter persuading the former to incentivise them via a carried interest, that is, a share of the returns above a certain level as measured by financial markets.[57]

This form of compensation was introduced into equity markets by private equity funds and hedge funds. The norm

---

57 Mihir Desai, 'The Incentive Bubble', *Harvard Business Review*, March 2012.

of the funds is the '2 and 20' rule whereby compensation is tied to the size of assets being managed (the 2 per cent) and to managers' performance as measured by the financial markets (the 20 per cent or 'carried interest'). It was a serious mistake that this form of compensation was so readily agreed by investors. It is difficult to justify commercially, and it creates a major misalignment of the interests of the two parties. If share prices are rising, the savers have to share the increases with the hedge funds and private equity funds, but if share prices drop, they have to absorb all the losses.

The impact of this form of compensation on the risk-taking of hedge funds and private equity funds was also not difficult to predict. They took risks knowing that if they generated huge returns they could take a large slice of them, but that if they failed someone else had to pick up the losses. And the performance of the funds did not in any way justify such a one-sided arrangement. Overall the private equity industry in the USA has underperformed a simple strategy of borrowing money and using it to buy a diversified portfolio of mid-cap stocks.[58]

In time the activities of the private equity funds and hedge funds, and the migration of talent from the investment banks to them, led to banks buying hedge funds and private equity funds, and launching their own funds, and to rewarding their best managers with contracts embodying the essential features of financial-market-based compensation. The large

58   Mihir Desai, ibid.

windfalls which resulted gave rise to a sense of entitlement which continues to this day.

This situation in which investment managers cream off large sums of money from the returns which should flow from companies to savers, and pay themselves large bonuses, cannot be allowed to continue. But what can be done to reverse it? One course of action would be for policy-makers to attempt to regulate the behaviour of investment managers. But, as Paul Woolley argues, bankers will strongly resist and actively seek to get around such regulations, which in any case it would be difficult to construct. Instead he suggests that a better way would be to encourage the giant funds to act to stop it, as they have every incentive to do so. The giant funds are the large pension, sovereign wealth, charitable and endowment funds around the world. If they could be persuaded to recognise the nature and extent of the problem – and change the way they contract and deal with agents – that would be the best solution.

To achieve this goal, he argues that the giant funds should adopt a number of policies, of which the most important are to take a long-term approach to investing based on long-term dividend flows rather than momentum-based strategies that rely on short-term price changes; to cap annual turnover of their portfolio at 30 per cent per annum; not to pay performance fees; and to insist on total transparency by managers with respect to their strategies, costs, leverage and trading.

At the same time, he argues, policy-makers and regulators worldwide should take steps to encourage adoption of these policies by giant funds. These include encouraging adoption by all public funds, withdrawing tax-exemption rights for all funds that fail to cap turnover, and the issue of GDP-linked bonds to encourage the adoption of GDP as a performance benchmark for funds as well as being an attractive proposition for investors and issuers alike. He also argues that regulations should not automatically approve financial products on the grounds that they enhance liquidity or complete markets.

If, by taking these actions, government could get funds to widely adopt the proposed policies, all funds would enjoy collective benefits in the form of more stable capital markets, faster economic growth, less appropriation by agents and less risk of crisis, and the ultimate reward achievable from both private and collective gains could, Paul Woolley calculates, be an increase of around 2–3 per cent in the real annual return of each fund.

I believe that Paul Woolley's proposed plan of action is on the right lines, but that it will take more than action by the giant funds to bring about the necessary changes. What is disgraceful is the way that savers generally have been exploited by investment managers, and this appropriation of wealth will only be stopped when all savers take action to force invest-ment managers to behave differently, and to act on behalf of the investors and not on behalf of themselves.

The government also has an interest in stopping this exploitation of savers if it wants to see the savings rate rise and people provide for their old age and retirement, and a Progressive government which has made fairness a key measure of its economic policies should see it as a major objective. I therefore think that the government should seek to mobilise the various bodies that represent shareholders to form a new Shareholders' Advisory Board to advise all shareholders on the way they should contract and deal with investment managers. If this involves the government providing some funds to the new body, then that would be a small price to pay for protecting savers. This new Shareholders' Advisory Board should be welcomed by people like the Trustees of Pension Funds, who must be aware that they have not produced good returns for their savers.

The new Shareholders' Advisory Board would have a responsibility for ensuring transparency and improved education for investors. To achieve transparency it would need to be able to require all the participants involved in investment management to give investors clear information about the fees they were being charged. The combination of transparency and education should put pressure on the participants in the investment management chain to cut their costs.

The new Shareholders' Advisory Board should also encourage all the bodies which hold the assets of savers fundamentally to alter the way they contract and deal with investment managers. In future the emphasis should be on investment based on an understanding of the fundamental value of the companies in which they invest, rather than on 'trading' based on the likely short-term movements of share prices. As I pointed out at the beginning of this chapter, competition between investment managers on the basis of relative performance is inherently a zero-sum game, and the investment management industry can benefit savers taken as a whole only to the extent that its activities improve the performance of investee companies.

The new Shareholders' Advisory Board should also encourage all the bodies which hold the assets of savers to do what the Kay Review advises:[59]

(i) Provide information to beneficiaries, including information on investment performance, in a way which is clear, timely, useable and relevant to clients' investment objectives.

(ii) Set mandates which focus investment managers on achieving absolute returns in line with beneficiary's long-term investment objectives, rather than short-term relative performance benchmarks, and encourage them to have more concentrated holdings.

(iii) Review the performance of investment managers at intervals no less than three to five years, and with reference to long-term absolute performance.

(iv) Encourage and empower investment managers to engage with investee companies as a means of improving company performance to deliver investment returns.

The last recommendation is very important when we look at the second principal–agent problem, which concerns the

---

59 'The Kay Review of UK Equity Markets and Long-Term Decision Making – Final Report', July 2012.

relationship between investment managers and firms – which we do now.

Corporate Governance

The second major principal–agent problem which arises from changes in the equity markets in the UK in the last fifty years concerns the relationship between investment managers and firms. This we will look at now because the efficiency of a country's system of corporate governance depends critically on how well the relationship between investment managers and firms works.

If we stand back and look at how the relationship between shareholders and firms has developed over the last fifty years in the UK, it is clear that it has worsened rather than improved. This is because the short-term investment strategies of many investment managers result in them having no interest in exercising their rights as shareholders, and as a result we have 'capitalism without owners'. As a defining characteristic of capitalism is the holding of the productive assets of a country by individuals who have a direct interest in making certain they are used efficiently over the long term, this is a major flaw.

As a result of the failure of investment managers to exercise their rights as shareholders, the system of corporate governance in the UK can be faulted on two grounds. Firstly, the nature and level of the incentives for corporate executives have been distorted by the use of a deeply flawed version of financial-markets-based compensation. Secondly, this had led to a large and extremely damaging financial-incentive bubble, which is unsustainable.

As a result of this form of compensation, the pay of top executives has soared in recent years, seemingly without any control. The average pay of the chief executives of Britain's FTSE 100 companies, for example, grew by more than 11 per cent per annum in real terms between 1999 and 2006, compared with 1.4 per cent for all full-time employees. In 2006, the average earnings of a top FTSE chief executive were nearly 100 times that of the average for all full-time employees. Twenty-five years earlier, it had been less than twenty-five times as high. Managerial talent is a vitally important ingredient in modern capitalism and should be richly rewarded in line with the contribution it makes to wealth creation, but managerial rewards should not be allowed to get out of control or to be based on a flawed form of compensation.

The version of financial-markets-based compensation used is flawed because it cannot be relied on in a simple way to compensate individuals fairly; this is due to the fact that it cannot easily disentangle skill from luck. In order for such financial-markets-based compensation to work successfully, executives should only be rewarded for success beyond that which would normally be expected. The CEO of an oil company should not be richly rewarded simply because the price of oil is sky rocketing up and all oil companies are making large profits. Instead, he should receive pay reflecting the return of his company less the returns of comparable firms in the industry. That would provide an incentive for high performance and a true measure of the incremental value of the executive.

But in recent years stock-option compensation has not been indexed to remove price appreciation that has arisen from market returns, with the result that managers received large rewards during a period of outstanding returns on asset markets. The situation was made worse by executives being allowed to manipulate the system by issuing options when share prices were low.

There are people who will argue that financial-markets-based compensation has brought about an alignment of the interests of managers and shareholders, but the reality is that in recent years mediocre stock market returns have paralleled very high levels of managerial compensation, and we have had a system which has rightly been called 'pay without performance'.

The second reason the UK system of corporate governance is flawed is that the failure of investment managers to exercise their rights as shareholders has resulted in little pressure on company executives to create and maintain competitive advantage in operating businesses by investing in product and process innovation as the only long-term source of shareholder value. Some poorly performing managers have been removed, many by takeovers, a tactic much approved of by investment bankers because of the huge fees involved, but not a good way of handling the problem. As the Kay Review points out, there is a substantial body of academic evidence which suggests that little or no value is added to business

171

by merger activity, and quarterly returns and the threat of a takeover bid are bound to make many corporate executives take a very short-term view of their company's performance.

An awareness of the problems which arise because the providers of capital and investment managers do not exercise their rights as owners has led in the last twenty years to the issue of a long series of corporate codes of conduct to try to remedy the situation. As a result of the collapse of a number of listed companies in 1990 and 1991, the first of these, the Cadbury Code, was issued in 1992.

This was a voluntary code of conduct for the boards of listed companies and contained two main provisions. Firstly, the chairman's role should in principle be separate from that of the chief executive, and the non-executive directors – that is, people who are not employed by a company but who sit on its board – should be given more power. Moreover, those non-executives ought to demonstrate independence from management. They should not be bankers, lawyers or other business people with whom the company does business or close friends or relatives of the chief executive or other senior managers. Also, a majority of the board ought to be such independent non-executive directors.

While the code was essentially a voluntary code, at its centre was a phrase that would occur in many corporate governance codes around the world: 'comply or explain'. Companies did not have to comply with the Cadbury recommendations, but if they did not they had to tell their shareholders why they had chosen not to do so. This also was voluntary, but a company might lose its listing on the London Stock Exchange if it failed to do so.

The Cadbury Code was followed by the Greenbury Report in 1995, which urged companies to disclose in their annual report details of how much key individuals earned; the Hampel Code in 1998, which reconsidered the Cadbury and Greenbury reports; the Turnbull Report in 1999, which discussed internal controls and risk management; and the Higgs Review in 2003, which strengthened some of the Cadbury recommendations only to see a few of its recommendations diluted in 2006 by the Financial Reporting Council.

While the various codes of conduct have formalised many key board processes, and made it more difficult for the chief executive of a company to run it to further his own interests, it is doubtful whether they have ultimately done much to improve the governance of UK companies, as the lack of control over executive salaries shows. The continuing failure of investment managers to get involved in the governance of the companies in which they invest has meant that non-executive directors of companies have been effectively appointed by the management of those companies and have not, therefore, been prepared to stand up to them when they believe that the company is not being managed as it should be. The emphasis of the codes of conduct has largely been on preventing the destruction of wealth rather than on its long-term creation, and they have been the cause, not surprisingly, of a considerable amount of pointless box-ticking.

There is a need, therefore, to keep this issue on the agenda of government. If the new Shareholders' Advisory Board can get all the organisations which hold the assets of savers to use their mandates to encourage and empower investment managers to engage with investee companies, that would be an enormous step forward. I would also like to see the Shareholders' Advisory Board facilitate and promote the use of nomination committees as they are used in Sweden.[60]

In looking at the use of nomination committees in Sweden, it is important to understand that there are key differences in the composition of Swedish and UK boards. In the UK, boards are unitary, bringing together executives and non-executives. In Sweden the board is primarily made-up of non-executives, and the CEO is sometimes but not always a member.

The use of nomination committees in Sweden was, interestingly, a Swedish response to the 1992 report of Sir Adrian Cadbury. They operate, however, in a very different way to nomination committees in the UK. In both systems nomination committees are the body with responsibility for finding the right people to serve on boards. In the UK the nomination committee is a sub-committee of the board. It is made up of board members and is usually chaired by the Chair of the Board. Board candidates are proposed by the nomination committee to the annual general meeting and in the normal course of events are elected.

In Sweden, on the other hand, the nomination committee

---

60 'Tomorrow's Corporate Governance: Bridging the UK engagement gap through Swedish-style nomination committees', Centre for Tomorrow's Company, 2010.

is a servant of the AGM. It is not made up of board members, but mainly of four or five of the largest owners of shares in the company. It has its mandate from the shareholders at the annual general meeting. It recommends to the shareholders at the annual general meeting who should join the board, the structure and amount of remuneration of each director, and procedural issues for the appointment of the following year's nomination committee. The remuneration of executive management is handled separately by the board.

If Swedish-type nomination committees were to be introduced into the UK they would, of course, have to be adapted to take account of the composition of UK boards. As I see it their main role would be to propose to the AGM who should be the non-executive directors of the board including the non-executive chairman, and to recommend the amount of remuneration they should receive. An internal nomination and remuneration committee, chaired by the non-executive Chair of the Board, and made up of non-executive directors, would nominate executive directors to the AGM and the remuneration they should receive. The nomination committee would also be the route through which shareholders could engage with the board on strategic issues.

There is nothing under the current 'comply or explain' arrangements of the UK's corporate governance code to stop a company listed in the UK from implementing such a UK version of the Swedish nomination committee, and the new Shareholders' Advisory Board I have proposed could facilitate and promote their use as a beneficial innovation to encourage stewardship by investment managers. Today the only way that investment managers can influence the board strategically or restrain it from paying itself disproportionate rewards is by reactive and ad hoc co-ordination with other shareholders. By contrast, a UK version of the Swedish nomination committee would give them a low-cost and proactive way of doing so.

It could be argued that in proposing that a UK version of the Swedish nomination committee should be tried out in the UK, I am putting forward something that goes against one of the central arguments of this book, which is that institutions should not be borrowed from other countries which have very different varieties of capitalism. But today there is not a great difference in the conditions under which the Swedish system of governance operates from those in the UK. In the 1980s a limited number of owners had control of many of Sweden's major listed companies, but this is no longer the case.

There are ways, therefore, that major investors can be encouraged to engage with companies and work with them more proactively than at present, and Progressive policymakers who want to create the best institutional conditions for companies to innovate and grow need both to get investment managers to engage more with investee companies, and to promote the use of Swedish nomination committees.

There is one other change that I believe should be made to improve both the functioning of equity markets and corporate governance in the UK, and that is to make takeovers more difficult. I would not want to stop them entirely, because there are occasions when putting two businesses together creates real synergy and added value. But as the Kay Review pointed out, there is a substantial body of academic evidence that suggests that little or no value is added to businesses by merger activity.

Takeovers and the threat of takeovers also do a great deal of harm. The threat of takeover, and the frequent reporting of performance, results in managers taking a short-term view and under-investing in physical assets or in intangibles such as product development, employee skills and reputation with customers. Secondly, because of the huge fees involved, takeover activity leads investment banks to focus on merger activity, which does little or nothing to create wealth. It also leads to a major misallocation of human resources, because many young managers and engineers who should be creating the new high-tech businesses of the future are attracted into the City by the huge salaries on offer and the opportunity to take part in exciting deals.

How can it be made more difficult to carry out such takeovers? Two simple changes could be made. The first is to raise the level of acceptances required from shareholders in the target company, and the second is to restrict voting in the target company to those who have held shares for more than a certain number of years. These moves would not stop takeovers which have the potential to create additional added value but they would hopefully, for example, stop the opportunistic buying of companies which are in the process of being turned around, and they would help the directors of a target company fight off any bid they believe would not contribute to the long-term success of their business. Combined with the removal of quarterly reporting obligations, I believe such moves would also encourage businesses to take a longer-term view.

In this chapter I have covered at great length the functioning of equity markets and corporate governance in the UK, both because their efficient functioning is important for economic growth and because a description of how they function and what can be done to make them function better illustrates three of the key themes of this book: that efficient institutions are essential for economic growth, that institutions have to be reformed to take account of changing circumstances, and that government has a key role to play in constructing and reforming those institutions.

SEVEN

BUILDING A KNOWLEDGE INFRASTRUCTURE

In Chapter 6, I looked at how well the UK's equity markets and system of corporate governance are functioning, and what reforms government needs to make to the underlying institutions in order to make them function better. In this chapter I will look at the second of the key tasks of government which I outlined in Chapter 4, namely, the building of the UK's knowledge infrastructure, which consists of its national system of innovation and its education and training system.

In the case of these two institutions I will, as in the case of UK equity markets and system of corporate governance, look first at what function we want them to perform, then at how efficiently they are currently performing it, and, finally, at what reforms the government should introduce to make them perform more efficiently.

The UK's National System of Innovation

The function of a country's national system of innovation is obviously to increase its rate of innovation. It is important to note, however, that here as elsewhere we are talking about innovation which increases the value-added of firms. A new type of financial engineering which enables private equity to extract more of the assets of a company which it has taken over, or a new type of tax planning which enables firms to avoid taxes, are simply types of wealth appropriation which should be discouraged rather than encouraged.

I only make this obvious point because when I was Minister of Science and Innovation in the last Labour government, I was told by one think-tank that there was a lot of 'hidden innovation' in our service industries. Leaving aside the question of how they knew about it if it was hidden, I asked for some examples, and was told solemnly, after some hesitation, that tax avoidance was an area where we are very innovative.

When the Labour government came to power in 1997, it found the UK's national system of innovation in a much neglected state. It was not seen as an essential part of any strategy for growth but as a group of responsibilities which the government had reluctantly to carry out, and the level of funding was disastrous. As a result there was a brain-drain of scientists to other countries, our scientific laboratories were in a very poor state of repair and lacking essential equipment, and the transfer of knowledge to industry and public policy was low. The quality of research done had, however, remained very high.

A major programme of reform was therefore launched by the Labour government when it came into power in 1997, which I developed during the eight years I was Minister of Science and Innovation from 1998–2006. This programme of reform was very wide-ranging and can be used to illustrate, I believe, how a national system of innovation can be improved so that it better performs its function. The main features of the UK's national system of innovation, and the changes that were made to it, can best be described under four headings. These are: the funding of research, knowledge transfer, the use of demand to stimulate innovation and the management of transitions.

Basic and Applied Research

A key input of any national system of innovation is the research done in industry, universities and government research institutes. Of these the most important is business enterprise R&D (BERD), as this correlates most closely with a country's innovation performance. In the UK as a share of GDP it is below the EU fifteen average, and has shown a slight downward trend, while most advanced economies have experienced fairly steady levels of R&D as a ratio of GDP since the turn of the century.

The difference in firm R&D intensity between the UK and other countries is at least in part the result of a different industrial structure. R&D intensive industries account for a smaller share of GDP in the UK than they do in some other countries, such as Germany, and hence overall R&D intensity will be lower even if R&D intensity within industries is comparable.

The UK performance must, however, be a cause for concern because it suggests that less innovation is taking place across the whole of industry. The last Labour government, therefore, introduced R&D tax credits in April 2000 for small and medium-sized enterprises (SMEs) and extended the scheme to other companies in April 2002. International evidence from OECD countries suggests that direct subsidies in the form of tax credits to private firms can help boost R&D, and the UK scheme is broadly considered to be a success.

A second key input to any national system of innovation is government-supported research, both basic research and applied or user-driven research. There are those who argue that there is no difference between the two, quoting Sir George Porter's remark that there are only two kinds of research, applied research and research which has not yet been applied. I think, however, that it is important to keep the distinction in mind because the best way to select, monitor and evaluate projects is very different for the two kinds of research.

In the case of basic research, the research projects should be selected by the scientists themselves, as only they can judge where the breakthroughs are likely to come. It is also difficult to be precise about the amounts of time and money necessary to complete the projects, and such projects are evaluated on the basis of papers published in prestigious journals and the citation of them by other researchers in their papers. On the other hand, applied research projects should be selected on the basis that they are most likely to meet the need of a particular user. It is also easier to say what amounts of money and time will be required to complete such projects, and projects should be evaluated in terms of whether they provide an answer to the user's need, and what increases in productivity or new products they produce.

There are also those that argue that government should support basic research because it is a 'public good', but that companies should be left to perform all applied research. On the other hand, some people argue that a country can get basic knowledge from anywhere in the world, and that governments should concentrate on funding the applied research that will be of most value to their national firms.

I believe that it is essential that governments support both kinds of research. The majority of radical innovations spring from basic research, and both national and foreign high-technology firms want to locate their operations, or parts of them, next to world-class research universities. The presence of such research is also necessary for training the next generation of researchers for industry. In the case of applied research, it is essential that most of it is funded by industry, as only industry is in a position to specify what is needed for success in the marketplace. But collaborative applied research is, like basic research, a public good in the sense that the value of the benefits cannot be completely captured by a single firm but spills over into the rest of society. Private firms left alone and seeking to maximise their returns will undertake less applied research than is economically optimal and collaborative applied research should, therefore, be supported by the government.

If we now look at the UK's institutions for funding and

carrying out basic research, we see that they are highly productive and produce world-class results.[61] The number of research papers published in journals and the number of subsequent citations of those papers are the two main indicators used to denote the scale and quality of research activity. In terms of volume the UK ranks third, attracting a share of world publications of 6.4 per cent, trailing only the USA and China. In terms of excellence, however, the UK accounts for the second largest share of citations after the USA: 10.9 per cent.

The UK also produces 14 per cent of the most cited 1 per cent of papers, trailing only the USA. Moreover, when the relative size of investment in R&D is accounted for, the UK research base achieves the best value for money among the large economies, leading on all counts of papers, citations and highly cited papers per pound spent on R&D.

Our universities are also highly regarded across the world. This is an area where the US leads the way but the UK is well placed in comparison to other major European countries. Shanghai's Jiao Tong University in its 2010 rankings of world universities had thirty-five US universities in the top fifty and just eleven from Europe, of which five were in the UK. The quality of the UK's basic research and universities should, therefore, be seen as a major economic asset of the country.

However, when the Labour government came into power in 1997, it found that the funding of the science base had been

---

61 'International Comparative Performance of the UK Research Base' (2011), Elsevier on behalf of BIS.

allowed to decline in comparison with other countries, and that the UK's research facilities were increasingly out-of-date and in a poor state of repair. A first priority, therefore, was to increase the funding for the science base. When the government came to power the science budget was £1.3 billion. As a result of substantial increases in a number of spending reviews, the science budget more than doubled in real terms by 2007/8. This included £500 million a year for the renewal of scientific facilities in universities. A fifteen-year roadmap for large facilities was also produced so as to provide the UK's world-class scientists with world-class scientific infrastructures.

Over the same period the Labour government also sought to improve the collaborative, applied R&D programmes supported by the government. In 1997 a few such programmes lingered on in the DTI administered by civil servants with little industrial or technological knowledge or experience. To improve the management of these programmes, in October 2004 the government established the Technology Strategy Board to manage the technology programmes of the DTI.

As a result of its early success the TSB was turned into an executive non-departmental public body (NDPB) in 2007. This gave it greater independence, the potential to make a consistent and more significant difference to the UK's innovation performance, and the ability to staff itself with people with industrial and technological knowledge and experience. A major programme of the TSB is one of collaborative, applied R&D. This is achieved through open competition for funding held every six months. The projects supported are part-funded by government and bring together business and other research partners to carry out research with a future commercial goal. By 2007 this programme had already proved to be highly successful. Over 600 user-driven collaborative R&D projects had already been approved for funding varying from £3,000 to £95 million. There was an average of five partner organisations per funded project, with small companies making up a third of the organisations involved. The 600 projects approved for funding at that stage represented over £900 million of R&D investment by government and business, with £465 million being committed by business and £435 being committed by government.

Also during 2011 and 2012, an evaluation was done of 400 collaborative R&D projects started after 2004 and finished in 2009:this showed an average return of £6.71 in additional gross value added per pound spent.

Knowledge Transfer

The second way that the Labour government sought to improve the UK's national system of innovation was by strengthening the links between research bodies and the commercial world. This is because collaboration has become an increasingly important part of innovation. The next layers of value creation, whether in technology, marketing or manufacturing are becoming so complex that no single firm can master them alone. As a result even a giant firm like IBM, which has tended in the past to be largely self-sufficient in its R&D, and which has greater resources than many small nation states, has had to enter into a whole series of collaborative arrangements in R&D. This is because no firm can now possibly cope single-handed with the full range of interrelated developments taking place as a result of the computer and telecommunications revolutions, and with the speed at which they are taking place.

As Joel Cowley, the head of IBM's strategic planning unit, has said:

> What we are seeing in so many different fields is that the next layers of innovation involve the intersection of very advanced specialities. The cutting edge of technical innovation in every field is increasingly specialised. Therefore, to come up with any valuable new breakthrough, you have to be able to combine more and more of these increasingly granular specialities. That is why collaboration is so important.[62]

It is also why a feature of the R&D scene in the 1980s has been a rapid proliferation of new agreements and consortia for collaboration in R&D, often international in scope.

The first area where the government sought to improve knowledge transfer was the universities. A lack of university knowledge transfer had been a great weakness of the UK's innovation system in the past. The government introduced a number of schemes to improve the UK's performance, and these appear to have produced a major cultural change within our universities, building capacity, increasing professionalism and making higher education institutions (HEIs) more

---

62   Thomas Friedman, *The World is Flat*, Penguin, 2005.

valuable partners for business. The schemes which the government introduced included 'The University Challenge Fund', which provided seed funds to universities, 'Science Enterprise Funds' to teach entrepreneurial skills to science and engineering undergraduates, and in 2001 the 'Higher Education Innovation Fund' (HEIF), to incentivise universities to transfer knowledge into industry and society. Into this last scheme the other two schemes were fairly quickly merged in order to simplify things for the universities. These schemes led to a dramatic increase in recent years in the amount of knowledge transfer from British universities, with the private sector putting a value of £3 billion on its collaborative and contract research with UK universities in 2009/10.

Table 7.1 Universities Working With Business

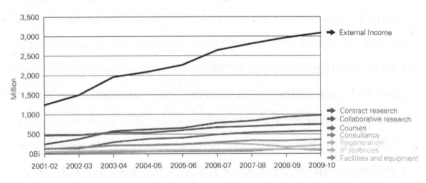

('Innovation and Research Strategy for Growth', Department for Business, Innovation and Skills, December 2011.)

In 2009/10, 273 spin-off companies were also created, some of which will add to the 969 university spin-offs that remained active three years after creation, and which, based on leading-edge research, turned over nearly £1.8 billion and employed around 17,000 people in that year.[63]

Table 7.2 Academic Spin-off Firms in the UK

	Number established	Number surviving After 3 years
2005-6	186	746
2006-7	226	844
2007-8	219	923
2008-9	215	976
2009-10	273	969

(Economics Paper No. 15, Department for Business, Innovation and Skills, December 2011.)

Limited data are available before 2000/01 as many HEIs did not monitor or record knowledge transfer performance until then. But between 1994 and 1999 a total of 338 were recorded (an average of seventy per annum). So a very substantial increase has taken place.

UK universities are also now doing well in comparison with American universities who are the leaders in this field. A Library House report in 2007 concluded 'UK universities are now producing spin-out companies of equivalent number and

---

63 Ibid.

quality to some of the USA's top institutions.'[64] The report compared the spin-out portfolios of a cross-section of UK universities with those of three top American universities, Stanford University, the University of Wisconsin (the world's sixteenth best research university according to the Shanghai Ranking System, with a technology transfer operation dating back to 1925) and the University of Washington (the world's seventeenth best research university according to the Shanghai Ranking System, located in a state that receives more than four times the venture-capital finance per head that the UK receives). Using external investment attracted as a proxy for quality, Stanford University came out top, but most of the UK universities performed well against the other two US universities.

The government also introduced a number of other knowledge transfer schemes, worth mentioning as they show the different ways that a government can encourage knowledge transfer in practical terms without directly intervening in firms' corporate strategies. Two of these schemes are managed by the Technology Strategy Board. The first of them is the set of knowledge transfer networks (KTNs) which the TSB set up. Each network is established in a specific field of technology or business application and brings together a variety of organisations such as businesses (suppliers and customers), universities, research and technology organisations, and the

---

64 'Spinning Out Quality: University Spin-Out Companies in the UK', Library House, March 2007.

finance community, to enable the exchange of knowledge and the stimulation of innovation in the network.

The purpose of the KTNs is to improve the UK's innovation performance by increasing the breadth and depth of knowledge transfer into UK-based businesses and by accelerating the rate at which this process occurs. One of the things that they have done is produce Technology Road Maps for emerging technologies which give a consensus picture of future technology developments and market needs, and which enable companies to focus their research efforts where they will have most value. KTNs have been set up in areas such as MNT (micro and nanotechnology), photonics, grid computing, low carbon and fuel cell technology, and cyber security.

The second major knowledge transfer programme set up by the TSB was one on emerging technologies which aims to foster business engagement with new technologies emerging from the UK science base at the earliest 'business readiness' stage. In each case businesses and leading academics are asked primarily via workshops what support might be appropriate. An action plan is then drawn up, and support is given in a variety of ways such as collaborative R&D competitions, user forums, technology showcasing, which provides academics with opportunities to 'pitch' their research and its potential to business, development of standards strategies and assessments of global market potential.

A third knowledge transfer initiative that the DTI set up was the Manufacturing Advisory Service which was launched in 2001 to provide help to small businesses with new manufacturing technology. This was based on the highly successful Manufacturing Extension Partnership (MEP) in the United States. The MEP, whose federal sponsor is the National Institute of Standards and Technology (NIST) within the US Department of Commerce, brings together a variety of technology and business providers to offer comprehensive, locally managed and demand-driven services to small and mid-sized manufacturers. This approach stands in contrast to the fragmented 'technology-push' methods that have characterised many previous federal technology transfer programmes. The MEP also typically employs industrially experienced field personnel who work directly with firms to identify needs, broker resources and develop appropriate assistance projects. The Manufacturing Advisory Service was modelled on the MEP and has been a great success. It also shows that institutions can be copied from countries that have a similar variety of capitalism.

In addition to these three knowledge transfer initiatives, the government also sought to strengthen high-tech clusters in the UK. We have seen that high-tech clusters can be an important source of growth, and the Library House Report, which has already been mentioned, showed that partly as a result of the Higher Education Innovation Fund, high-tech clusters have been forming around our world-class research universities. World-class research universities not only promote innovation and entrepreneurship by spinning out companies but also create an appropriate micro-environment to attract innovation-based companies and foreign R&D facilities. In fact there is a strong correlation between the score a university receives as a result of the national Research Assessment Exercise (RAE) and the number of venture backed companies around it (see Chart 7.1).

Chart 7.1 University RAE Rating vs. Venture-Backed Companies

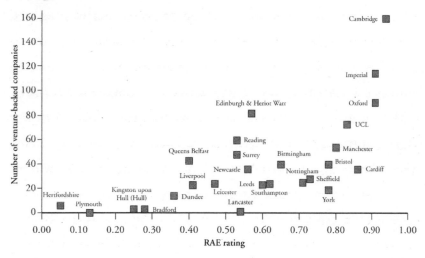

('The Race to the Top: A Review of Government's Science and Innovation Policies', HM Treasury, 2007.)

The fact that the high-tech clusters in the UK have grown up around our world-class research universities should not come as a surprise to anyone, though it does come as a surprise to those politicians who think that knowledge transfer only takes the form of applied research. If one asked a person knowledgeable about American universities to list the universities which have had the most beneficial impact on their local economies they would probably mention Stanford, MIT, Berkley, Austin (Texas) and Duke University in North Carolina, all of which are, of course, world-class research universities.

The government also sought in a number of other ways to support the development of high-tech clusters, without making the mistake of trying to impose a plan on where they should go. For example, early in its life it allocated £50 million to support the setting up of high-tech incubators. It also developed a plan to concentrate its major research facilities on two Science and Innovation Campuses, at Harwell near Oxford and at Daresbury outside Manchester, and to support UKCMRI, the UK Centre for Medical Research and Innovation, a joint project in London of the Medical Research Council, Cancer Research UK, the Wellcome Trust and University College, London. Each of these projects was seen to have the potential to become the centre of a high-tech cluster.

The Demand for Innovation

It is easy for governments to see ways in which they can influence the supply side of a country's national system of innovation, but less easy for them to see what they can do on the demand side. But there is one very important way that they can do so, and that is to use the government's purchases of goods and services to stimulate innovation. The government in the UK is in a very good position to do so because the size of its procurement budget (roughly £220 billion a year, about 15 per cent of GDP) is by many orders of magnitude more important for innovation policy than most innovation policy instruments, even if only a fraction is spent on innovation activity. Government demand as a share of total demand in 2008 was 35 per cent for pharmaceuticals, 29 per cent for medical and precision instruments, 13 per cent for aircraft and spacecraft and 10 per cent for computer services.

All too often government departments procure these goods and services on the basis of out-of-date specifications and lowest cost tenders, as this is the least risky way of doing so. It is also the easiest way because the government cannot be accused of favouring one supplier over another. But by being an intelligent customer, by engaging suppliers early in the procurement process, by combining this early involvement with contracts based on well-defined outcomes, by being less risk-averse, and by making use of Grand Challenge competitions, government can use its procurement to drive innovation in the economy. Government departments can also use user-driven R&D to stimulate innovation in the economy, and in 2001 the Labour government launched the Small Business Research Initiative (SBRI), modelled on the highly successful Small Business Innovation Research (SBIR) programme in the USA. The latter programme was established in 1982, at a time when a failure to translate the USA's research prowess into commercial advantage was held to be undermining US competitiveness, and it is generally agreed that the SBIR has played an important part in sustaining the demand for new products and services in the US economy. Each year, on average, over 4,000 awards are made under the scheme to US small businesses, worth over $2 billion in total.

At first the Small Business Research Initiative (SBRI) in the UK was not a success. A target of 2.5 per cent of external government R&D to be spent on SME's was established, but government departments largely spent this on pieces of research relating to the development of policy. In April 2009, however, the Technology Strategy Board having taken over its administration, the programme began to perform the function it was originally intended to perform, which is to issue R&D procurement contracts to develop new and innovative products and services in areas where government departments believe that innovation can help the public sector do its job better. Since the re-launch of the SBRI there have been eighty-two SBRI competitions run with twenty-six separate public sector organisations and over £60 million of contracts issued. The competitions have helped small and micro businesses to engage with government departments, and the validation effect of having a government contract has helped a number to raise venture capital or other additional financing. This is another example of how institutional mechanisms can successfully be copied from another country with a similar variety of capitalism.

Managing Transitions

A final way in which governments can improve their national systems of innovation is by helping them move across technology divides. Technological divides offer tremendous opportunities for innovation and growth, but they also have a very destabilising effect on broad societal agreements, such as the notion of property and the competitive position of firms, as new entrants take advantage of the new technology to challenge incumbents. For these reasons, economies cannot generally cross such divides on their own, and the state has to help them to do so.

A typical example of such a technological divide is the digital revolution. We are all currently living through this. It is easiest to look at how the state inevitably got involved by examining the situation in the United States where the digital revolution initially had the biggest impact. If we look at the United States, we see that as well as funding the basic research that created the digital revolution, and in many cases promoting the necessary technological infrastructure, the state has also had to establish the fictitious commodity of information through intellectual property rights, and embed digital markets in social norms. Far from being neutral, these interventions clearly have political effects.

At the start of the digital revolution, the American government relied heavily on self-regulating groups to establish and sustain markets in cyberspace. This policy very much coincided with the views of the 'Net' pioneers who were forging the system rules and building the architecture of the early internet. They saw government as an intruder and believed that the architecture of the internet made it impossible to regulate. John Gilmore, an early internet advocate, claimed that 'the Net interprets censorship as damage and routes around it',[65] and this view epitomised the beliefs of many of the early technologists.

---

65 John Zysman and Abraham Newman, 'The State in the Digital Economy', in Jonah D. Levy (ed.), *The State After Statism*, Harvard University Press, 2006.

However, this early view that the internet should be free of government was completely unrealistic. As soon as the internet began to be used for commerce, the need for a legal structure for it became obvious. The issue was no longer a technical one of how to operate a network but how to operate a marketplace, and appropriate rules had to be designated for everything from intellectual property to taxation. The results of these rules were bound to have distributional and political consequences, and there was no way that the state could hand over its responsibilities in these areas to private actors.

As a result we find, for example, the American government passing the Digital Millennium Copyright Act of 1998, which rebuilt walls around the intellectual property rights of content providers ranging from Hollywood to the publishing industry. This was done by creating penalties for the circumvention of encryption programs, and outlawing the manufacture or sale of code-breaking software. The state also became heavily involved in issues of privacy and harmful content.

This involvement of the state in creating the rules of the digital revolution after an initial period of freedom from state intervention should not, however, have come as a surprise. History tells us of many occasions when new technology has initially been seen as challenging government's authority and pioneers have rushed forward to declare the death of the state, only to be followed by a period when the government is required to intervene to create a new set of rules for the technology. This is because, as Debora Spar has written, 'Governments provide the property rights that entrepreneurs eventually want, the legal structures that commerce craves, and the stability that society demands.'[66]

As she has also shown, we can see the same pattern in transoceanic voyages in the seventeenth century, made possible by advances in shipbuilding and navigational devices, and in radio at the beginning of the twentieth century, as we are now seeing in cyberspace. When technology reveals a space, as it did in each of these cases, which for practical purposes had not been there before, those who have created it often find it difficult to conceive of it being governed. How could anyone in the seventeenth century imagine that order could be imposed on the vast seas or in the air at the beginning of the twentieth century? But in each of these cases, the new technology went through four distinct phases: innovation, commercialisation, creative anarchy and rules.

These cases also illustrate how markets get established, and how business and government shape their creation. It is a failure of much political economy in recent years that business and government are seen as belonging to wholly different spheres, whereas what these historical events illustrate is that markets are institutions which have to be embedded by government in rules if they are to operate effectively.

The Coalition Government's Strategy

The coalition government which came into power in 2010 could very easily have taken the view that the science budget

---

66   Debora L. Spar, *Ruling the Waves*, Harcourt Inc., 2001.

had done very well during the previous thirteen years and should, therefore, be cut back in line with other government spending in order to reduce the government deficit. But it maintained the £4.6 billion ring-fenced science and research programme funding. And while it cut back the spending on capital budgets, since 2010 it has allocated a further £495 million to them. Admittedly, this was at a time when a number of other governments were increasing their research budgets as part of stimulus packages, but it was nevertheless a far-sighted move.

Then in 2011 the Department of Business, Innovation and Skills issued a policy document, 'Innovation and Research Strategy for Growth', together with a background paper summarising the economic thinking on which the policy paper was based. This policy document also represented some new, important thinking by the coalition government. It argued that a large body of evidence shows that innovative economies are more productive and faster growing, and, therefore, stated that improving the UK's innovation performance was an essential component of the government's growth plan. At the same time it bought into the concept of the UK's innovation ecosystem which had first been set out in the report 'The Race to the Top', which I had written for the previous government, and it described the innovation ecosystems of global innovation leaders such as the US, Japan, Germany and Sweden. The policy document also envisaged the government playing a key role in developing the innovation ecosystem. 'The government', it stated, 'recognises the role of the innovation ecosystem in growing our knowledge economy and is committed to maximising its value'.

Finally, it rightly described the innovation ecosystem as covering, in addition to firms, research active universities, the Technology Strategy Board, the Intellectual Property Office, the Design Council, the Research and Innovation Campuses, and what it described as innovation infrastructure organisations such as the National Measurement Office, the National Physical Laboratory, the British Standards Institution and the UK Accreditation Service.

This adoption of the concept of the national innovation ecosystem was very important. The policy document also announced that the government was making a number of key investments in line with it. These covered three areas, a national network of technology and innovation centres, emerging technologies, and open data and transparency. These investments are of interest because they are all examples of targeted resourcing, that is, resourcing intended to focus the energies of scientists and engineers on a particular set of tasks, and create synergies by getting groups of highly skilled people working together to achieve a goal of national importance.

The network of intermediate research bodies which had existed in the UK had been allowed to run down in the years of the Conservative government from 1979 to 1997, and the Labour government had only put money into new ones on a very haphazard basis. In putting money into establishing an elite national network of technology and innovation centres, operating under the brand name of Catapult Centres, the coalition was, therefore, filling an important gap in the UK's national system of innovation. The aim of these centres is to provide comprehensive access to specialist capability and expertise, in order to transform innovative ideas and technologies rapidly into valuable products, processes and systems.

The government announced that the Technology Strategy Board would invest over £200 million in six centres, with the network completed in 2013. The first centres would be in High Value Manufacturing, which largely consisted of already existing centres, cell therapy and offshore renewable energy. Subsequently it unveiled plans for four more Catapult Centres to focus on satellite applications, the connected digital economy, future cities and transport systems.

The second area where the government announced it was making a major investment was emerging technologies. On the basis of a robust analytical framework drawing on a wide range of expertise, the government announced that four technology areas had been prioritised: synthetic biology, energy efficient computing, energy harvesting and the material graphene which had been discovered in Manchester in 2001 by 2010 Nobel Physics Laureates Andre Geim and Konstantin Novoselov. These areas had been selected on the basis of five key criteria: the potential size of the global market and its rate of growth; the range of applications of the technology across a number of economic sectors; the capability of the research base to develop these technologies and the number and strength of UK companies and supply chains relative to international competitors; and the ability of the UK to capture and protect the value created by patenting, embedding and exploiting intellectual property.

The Technology Strategy Board would focus on synthetic biology, energy efficient computing and energy harvesting, while £50 million would be invested in the development of a Graphene Global Research and Technology Hub to develop commercial applications for graphene.

The third area of investment highlighted in the policy document was that of open data and transparency. The government announced that it would open up access to core public datasets on transport, weather and health, including giving individuals access to their online GP records by the end of the current Parliament, and that it would provide up to £10 million over five years to establish an Open Data Institute to help industry exploit the opportunities created through the release of this data.

As a policy document 'Innovation and Research Strategy for Growth' is important and far-sighted, but it has two weaknesses and those will need to be tackled in the future. The first is the role of government departments, and the use they make of their R&D expenditures. These are very substantial. The civil departments other than BIS spend about £1.5 billion per annum on research, and the Ministry of Defence spends about £2 billion on development and research. While a great deal of effort has gone into improving the effectiveness of other parts of the UK's national system of innovation, not enough effort has gone into improving the use of the research funds of government departments.

The reasons why this is the case are not difficult to find. The use to which the funds should be put has never in recent years been clearly stated. Are they to be used simply to inform the policy development of departments or should they be used to support innovation in the industries and communities with which government departments are engaged? Secondly, there has never been any pressure from the centre of government on departments to get them to use their funds to drive and support innovation in the national interest. And, thirdly, because the funds are not ring-fenced, they have constantly been raided when times are hard to deal with overspends in other parts of departments.

The neglect of this part of the UK's national system is a missed opportunity. As we have already seen in Chapter 6, government departments in the USA use targeted resourcing of scientific and technological research to advance new technologies in the business community, whereas in the UK there have only been a few attempts, such as the creation of the Office for the Strategic Co-ordination of Health Research by the Department of Health, and the support given by the Ministry of Defence to its contractors, to use the funds of a government department to support innovation in industry.

Also the policy document itself mentions a number of areas such as the energy, water and agri-food industries which make an important contribution to UK industry, and which could benefit massively from government departments supporting innovation in them. The policy document seems to envisage the Technology Strategy Board taking action to support innovation in these industries, but I think it is time to tackle this issue directly by ring-fencing the research funds of government departments, by making it clear that they should be used to drive and support innovation in the industries and communities with which the departments are involved, and by embedding R&D units, which are staffed by scientists and engineers with commercial experience, in the relevant government departments. It will be necessary, however, if this is to happen, for a major political initiative to be taken by the Prime Minister at the centre of the government because, as we will see in Chapter 9, there is no other way that Whitehall could deliver such a change.

The second area of weakness in the policy document is its treatment of the regional dimension of science and innovation. The coalition's hasty abolition of the Regional Development Agencies and their replacement with the powerless and penniless Local Enterprise Partnerships was clearly a serious mistake. The Regional Development Agencies suffered from not having a clear mission, from being poorly supervised by Whitehall, and from being set up in some cases in parts of the country where they were not needed. But their abolition means that government now has no way of delivering a regional policy with a technological dimension.

There are two obvious options which could be looked at in order to correct this mistake. These are the creation of Regional Development Agencies in parts of the country which need them, or alternatively opening three or four regional branches of the Technology Strategy Board. Which of these would be the best solution will depend on the regional economic policy that a future government develops.

While the Innovation and Research Strategy for Growth has some weaknesses, it is an extremely important document as it establishes a consensus around the concept of a national innovation ecosystem, and the importance of the government supporting it. Future governments, if they want to be credible, will need to ensure that they have the knowledge and analytical skills to improve its performance rather than indulging in ideological irrelevancies.

The Education and Training System

It might be thought that it would be easy to state what function we want the education and training system of our country to perform, but it turns out that there is a wide range of views on its purpose. There are many teachers and educationalists who believe that the main aim of schools and universities should be to enable children to 'realise their potential' as individuals in some unspecified way, and that it is not to produce, as they would describe it, 'fodder for industry'. In this world careers advice and the supply of labour market information to inform young people's educational choices are of little importance, and what proportion of young people take which subject at school and university is not of much interest.

I believe, however, that work is central to most people's lives, and that if they are to lead fulfilling ones they need, while at school and university, to be able to acquire the knowledge and skills that will enable them to get jobs which they believe are socially useful and which will make full use of their abilities, and also to have access to good careers advice and labour market information. A world in which, for example, there are many able young people who are unskilled and unemployed, while the economy is desperately short of technicians, is a world which, as far as I am concerned, the education and training system is failing.

However, when I was Minister of Science and Innovation in the last government I had the strong impression that the Department of Education and Skills was almost totally uninterested in the subjects that young people were taking at school or university, and had little interest in the fact that there was a huge unfilled demand for technicians in the economy. They were barely aware that there was a general drift downwards in the number of young people doing scientific A levels, and that there had been a fifteen-year decline in the number of young people doing Physics A level, and when the latter figure was pointed out to them they were not able to give an explanation. This was an extremely worrying situation at a time when our economy is increasingly dependent on scientific and technological knowledge and skills.

We, therefore, in the Department of Trade and Industry did a great deal of work to turn the situation around. This involved cutting back the vast number of small, underfunded schemes to encourage young people to do so-called STEM subjects (science, technology, engineering and mathematics), and introducing two major new national schemes. The two new schemes were the Science and Engineering Ambassadors

Scheme which supports young scientists and engineers in industry and research to go into schools to tell the young people about the exciting work that they do, and a scheme to put after-school science and engineering clubs into all secondary schools.

These initiatives have been warmly welcomed by schools and today there are 25,000 individuals approved as Ambassadors and available to work with schools and colleges. Also, very encouragingly 40 per cent of the Ambassadors are female and 60 per cent are under the age of thirty-five. Today there are also 2,400 state secondary schools signed up to the STEM Club network, representing over 60 per cent of such schools in the UK.

Also research showed that the decline of young people taking Physics A level started at the same time as the introduction of Double Science at GCSE level, and so we encouraged schools to return to Triple Science. This meant that young people were once again able to take Physics, Biology and Chemistry as separate subjects, instead of doing double science which gave them a mix of all three. A second factor accounting for the shortage of young people doing A level Physics was an appalling shortage of qualified Physics teachers, and we, therefore, sought to get the Department of Education to step up their recruitment efforts.

A final initiative was to encourage industry, schools and other bodies to bring together many of their science and engineering enrichment activities and prize presentations at one big national fair each year. This has been a huge success. In 2009, 8,000 people attended the first Big Bang Fair. Just two years later, in 2011, this number had risen to an impressive 29,000, and in 2012 the fair held in Birmingham attracted 56,000 visitors.

As a result of all these initiatives the numbers of young people taking STEM A levels has improved significantly. Between 2006 and 2011 the numbers taking Physics and Chemistry A levels increased by around 25 per cent. Mathematics is up a remarkable 50 per cent, with 75,000 people taking A level maths in England last year, though this is partly due to special circumstances which reduced it at the start of the period. A level Further Mathematics also continues its year-on-year rise due to the introduction of an on-line course, with over 11,000 entries in 2011 – a 75 per cent increase in five years.

And there is hope that all these A level numbers will continue to rise as more and more fourteen and fifteen-year-olds opt for triple science at GCSE. Numbers studying Biology, Chemistry and Physics as three separate GCSE subjects have risen from 46,000 in 2006 to 135,000 in 2011.

The Supply of Technicians

If we see a main function of the education and training system as being to give all young people the knowledge and skills to enable them to get jobs which will make full use of their abilities, then one of its biggest flaws is the many vacancies for technicians at a time when many young people who have the ability to fill them are unemployed. In its 2010 National Strategic Skills Audit, the UK Commission for Employment and Skills highlighted an urgent need for technicians within sectors of high economic importance, including manufacturing, oil, gas, electricity, chemicals, pharmaceuticals, automotive, engineering and broadcasting. And in OECD comparisons of thirty countries, the UK scores eleventh on 'high' but only twentieth on 'intermediate skills'. Also, many studies over the years have shown the harmful effect this lack of technician skills has on UK productivity.

This situation has existed for a century, during which time we have looked enviously at the German system. We have repeatedly sought to improve our system of technician training without realising that this is very difficult to do without the effective trade associations and trade unions that Germany has.

In Germany the trade associations set the standards for technicians, and put pressure on their members to train apprentices and refrain from poaching. In the UK trade associations are too weak and underfunded to take on these roles, and so we have to devise our own solution.

There are three institutional components of an effective system of technician training and education. They are a well-understood system of qualifications for transferable technician skills which works in the marketplace, a system of funding young people while they acquire the qualifications, and the teachers and facilities to train the young people. A well-understood system of qualifications which works in the marketplace is required because young people will not undertake a rigorous course of study unless they know that the qualifications that they acquire at the end of it, if they are successful, will mean that they can get a job with better pay and security. Also most young people do not have the resources to pay for a lengthy course of study, and obviously, if there are no good teachers or facilities available, they cannot acquire the necessary skills. All these three attributes exist in Germany, but are largely absent in the UK.

However, in the final months of the last Labour government I managed to persuade it to support the setting-up of a scheme which has the potential to provide in the UK the three institutional components of an effective system of technician training and education. This is based on using the professional institutions which cover the scientific, medical, ICT and engineering areas. They have high prestige in the UK, they have a considerable knowledge of educational standards, which they are able to impose on their members, and in a few cases they already have a registered technician qualification.

A Technician Council has been set up and this is working with the professional bodies to produce a common, national registered technician qualification. Courses which cover all the ground necessary to gain this qualification, or which do so subject to the trainee gaining some extra piece of knowledge or experience, will be designated as such. Young people will, therefore, be able to take courses knowing that they will lead to a qualification which has credibility in the marketplace.

At the same time the Baker Dearing Trust has initiated the setting up of a number of so-called University Technical Colleges. These are state-funded schools, very loosely attached to universities, which are essentially technical colleges which take pupils on at fourteen and give them a technical and practical education. The curriculum they teach will be aligned with the technical knowledge and experience necessary to become a registered technician.

This is an exciting educational development because it opens up the possibility of making a technical stream a key part of our school system, the absence of which has been a major failure of our education and training system for a long time, and of providing the second and third of the institutional components which I have argued are essential if a country is to have an effective system of technician education and training.

If, however, the Registered Technician Scheme is going to have a major impact it will need the government to support it by reforming Further Education Colleges. This is an area which has long been neglected by governments. As a result, the Colleges do not have a clear mission, providing as they do a mixture of remedial education, adult education and technician-level knowledge and training. Their funding system also has a number of flaws. Because it is done on an annual cycle, teaching staff are mainly on short-term contracts, which does not make for a high level of teaching. The colleges are also poorly equipped, and the funding doesn't ensure that the colleges are closely linked to local industry needs, which is essential for this type of education and training.

In all these areas a reforming government will need to make changes if it wants to provide more opportunities for young people who are not going to university to get skilled jobs. It should make clear that the central mission of FE Colleges is to provide young people with technician-level knowledge and skills. It should put the funding on a triennial basis, it should provide funds so that the colleges are properly equipped, and it should make the funding of the colleges dependent on them providing plans closely linked to the needs of local industry.

Finally, a reforming government will need to put careers advice and labour market information firmly on its agenda. In spite of all the talk about the need to raise the aspirations of young people the level of careers advice in the UK is poor. And to the extent that governments have addressed it they have tended to make it worse. Mrs Thatcher privatised the careers advice service. The Labour government then renamed it Connexions and required it to give advice on all the problems young people face, and to focus particularly on NEETs, that is, young people who are not in education, employment or training, and the current coalition has abolished Connexions, only putting a vague requirement on schools to provide careers advice in whatever way they think best.

It is an appalling story which reflects well on no one, and some serious thought now needs to be given to what is the best combination of in-house knowledge and bought-in services to help young people in schools and universities to choose the careers which will make best use of their abilities and which they think are valuable to society, and which will, therefore, give them the greatest sense of self-fulfilment.

There is also a need to provide better labour market information to schools and universities to enable them to better align the courses they offer young people with the needs of the labour market, and to enable young people to make better decisions about the courses they take and the career choices they make. This is not about manpower planning, but it is about telling young people about the current state of the labour market, where there are vacancies for well-paid jobs with good prospects, and what knowledge and skills they need to acquire in order to apply for them.

A Higher Level of Policy-Making

If the type of institutional reform described in this chapter and the previous one is to be made, then it will require a much higher level of policy-making from politicians and civil servants. It is very easy to develop policies which say that as a matter of ideology the state should take over some activity, or alternatively that some activity should be outsourced or privatised. But what politicians and policy-makers now require is the ability to analyse their country's economic institutions and propose reforms, a much more difficult task.

As I hope I have shown in this chapter and the previous one, it is possible to say what function we want a specific institution to perform, to analyse whether it is performing that function efficiently, and to seek to reform it if it isn't. We can also make rational decisions about whether to import institutions from other countries. But if this is to be done successfully, then the quality of policy-making by politicians and civil servants will need to be improved.

At the current time what is described in government as

policy-making is often nothing of the sort, being simply the production of documents which describe what needs to be done to implement a minister's policies. Policy-making in the sense of reviewing the performance of a specific institution against an agreed objective, generating ideas about different reforms which could be made to it, and evaluating the different reforms in terms of their cost and effectiveness, is fairly rare. But the institutions with which we are dealing in this book are complex ones, and there are many vested interests, and if a future government is going to be successful in reforming the UK's economic institutions then the quality of policy-making by politicians and civil servants will need to be significantly better.

EIGHT

PROGRESSIVE CAPITALISM AND THE DEVELOPING WORLD

The theories of development economists since the Second World War have followed a similar path to the theories of economists seeking to understand and accelerate growth in the developed world. In developed countries the interwar development of Keynesian economics, and the rapid industrialisation of the USSR under the socialist central planning system, led to a dramatic swing of economic theory and practice towards intervention in the immediate post-war years. It also led to the adoption by many developed countries of interventionist policies, such as the nationalisation of industry and indicative planning.

In the quarter-century after the Second World War the state also took a more active role in many less developed countries. Their desire to achieve economic independence from their colonial masters, as well as political independence, put economic development at the top of their agendas, and it was widely believed that the best way to attain this goal was state-led industrialisation.

To justify this state-led industrialisation and the use of tariff protection to grow new industries, the traditional infant industry argument was evoked as well as an array of new theories to support the co-ordination of industrial investment. Post-war development thinking was heavily influenced by the 'big push' model of economists who stressed the demand complementarity between different industries, and the need, therefore, for investment co-ordination by the state.

The ideas of Gerschenkron, who based his theories on the earlier experiences of European industrialisation, were also very influential. He highlighted the interaction of the growing minimum efficient scale of production and the under-development of financial institutions in developing countries, and argued that as a country embarks on the development process later and later it needs to raise proportionally bigger and bigger amounts of savings, and the state, therefore, has to become involved.

Also, in the same way that state intervention in the developed world fell dramatically in the 1970s, the developing countries experienced a major fall in the 1980s, and by the end of that decade a set of neo-liberal policy principles had emerged, commanding wide support, which the economist John Williamson in 1990 unhappily called 'the Washington Consensus'. These principles are listed below and have largely remained at the core of conventional development thinking since then.

Table 8.1 Original Washington Consensus

1	Fiscal discipline	6	Trade liberalisation
2	Re-ordering public expenditure priorities	7	Liberalisation of inward foreign direct investment
3	Tax reform	8	Privatisation
4	Liberalising interest rates	9	Deregulation
5	A competitive exchange rate	10	Property rights

(John Williamson, A Short History of the Washington Consensus, in the Washington Consensus Reconsidered, Oxford University Press, 2008.)

Towards the end of the 1990s, this list was supplemented with a series of so-called second generation reforms which were institutional in nature and focused on problems of 'good governance', but 'the Washington Consensus' remained a statement of 'market fundamentalism', the view that markets solve most, if not all, economic problems by themselves. According to Williamson, 'The Washington Consensus was a … response to a leading role for the state in initiating industrialisation and import substitution. The Washington Consensus said that era was over.'[67]

If we now look at what impact these policies have had, we find that the developing countries experienced a similar decline in the growth of per capita income between 1960 to 1980 and 1980 to 2000 as the developed world did, with the

---

[67] Narcis Serra, Shari Spiegel and Joseph E. Stiglitz, 'Introduction: From the Washington Consensus Towards a New Global Governance' in Narcis Serra and Joseph E. Stiglitz (ed.), *The Washington Consensus Reconsidered*, Oxford University Press, 2008.

growth of per capita income in the developing world decelerating from 3 per cent to 1.5 per cent between the same two periods. And if we subtract the significant acceleration of growth in China and India in the latter period due to their major reforms then the rate in that period is reduced by 1 per cent. Per capita income in Latin America almost stood still in the 1980 to 2000 period and in sub-Saharan Africa it shrank.

Furthermore if we look at the policies of successful countries in the developing world during this period we do not find that their policies correspond with those championed by the 'Washington Consensus'. If we take the policies of South Korea and Taiwan, for example, we find that they exhibit very strong differences from the mainstream consensus. Neither country undertook significant deregulation or liberalisation of its trade and financial systems until well into the 1980s. They both relied heavily on public enterprise, and South Korea did not even welcome direct foreign investment. And they both made use of a wide range of industrial policies such as directed credit, trade protection, export subsidisation, tax incentives and other non-uniform interventions, of the sort deplored by the 'Washington Consensus'.

At the same time Latin America, which adopted many of the 'Washington Consensus' policies, did poorly when compared with East Asia. Countries such as Mexico, Argentina, Brazil, Columbia, Bolivia and Peru did a great deal of liberalisation, deregulation and privatisation, and yet Latin America's growth rate has remained a fraction of its pre-1980 level. A similar though smaller puzzle exists in the case of Africa where economic decline persisted in spite of its adopting some of the 'Washington Consensus' policies. At the end of this chapter, having looked at why some developing countries grow faster than others, I will seek to explain why East Asia grew faster than Latin America, by comparing Brazil with South Korea in detail.

The Nurturing of Infant Industries

If we see the accumulation by firms of organisational and technological capabilities as a key process of economic growth then the need for firms to acquire economies of scale and learn-by-doing before they are exposed to the full force of international trade becomes obvious. If new industries are not protected they will be wiped out before they have achieved the cost reductions which come from economies of scale and learning-by-doing, even though in the long-term they could be very profitable.

In such cases market signals will not encourage firms to accumulate the organisational and technological capabilities they need to acquire in order to enter new higher-value-added industries, and they will only do so if they receive active government support in the catch-up process in the form of protection and direct and indirect subsidies. Safeguarding the possibility of learning is the fundamental and best reason for protecting infant industries.

It should be noted, however, that such policies to nurture infant industries can lead to a protected, inefficient home industry. To be successful, governments have to balance measures aimed at capability building with measures to curb wealth appropriation and inertia. As we shall see later in this chapter, the great success of the countries of East Asia in the last fifty years is that they have developed policies which achieve both these objectives.

If anyone doubts the need for developing countries to nurture infant industries they have only to look at the historical record. We have already seen how Japan enabled some of its industries, including its car industry, to become internationally competitive by protecting them, and we will see later in this chapter how countries like South Korea and Taiwan used tariffs and entry restrictions to build up the organisational and technological capabilities of firms in key industries.

It is also the case that today's developed countries did not get rich through the neo-liberal policies and institutions that they recommend to developing countries today. This is not, of course, the orthodox version of the economic history of today's developed countries which emphasises the benefits of free trade and laissez-faire industrial policies. According to this view of history, from the eighteenth century onward the industrial success of laissez-faire Britain proved the superiority of free-market and free-trade policies.

The historical reality is very different.[68] Starting in 1721, the British government introduced a series of policies aimed at promoting manufacturing. This included raising the duties on imported foreign manufactured goods and extending export

---

68   Ha-Joon Chang, *Kicking Away the Ladder*, Anthem Press, 2003.

subsidies (bounties) to new items like silk products (1722) and gunpowder (1731), while the existing export subsidies to sailcloth and refined sugar were increased (in 1731 and 1733 respectively). They would never, of course, have got away with such an appalling distortion of trade if the World Trade Organization had been in existence.

In the second half of the eighteenth century, Britain began to increase the technological lead it had over its competitors, but it did not stop its policy of industrial promotion until the mid-nineteenth century, by which time it had an overwhelming lead. In 1820 its average tariff rates at 45–55 per cent were probably the highest in the world. There was a round of tariff reductions in 1833, but the big change only came in 1846 when the Corn Laws were repealed and tariffs on many manufactured goods were abolished. The UK became a champion of free trade but only after it had become a world technological leader behind high and long-lasting tariff barriers.

The USA pursued a similar infant industry strategy. During the nineteenth century the USA was both the fastest growing economy in the world and the most protectionist for most of it. Also, in the same way that the UK only liberalised its trade and became a champion of free trade after it had achieved a world technological lead in the mid-nineteenth century, so the United States only liberalised its trade and became a champion of free trade after the Second World War when it had achieved global industrial supremacy.

It is also worth noting that the change of policy in both these cases had been predicted by Friedrich List who believed in free trade but who thought it could only be achieved when countries were almost equal in terms of wealth and technology. In his book *The National System of Political Economy*, originally published in 1841, he wrote:

> It is a very common clever device that when anyone has attained the summit of greatness, he kicks away the ladder by which he has climbed up, in order to deprive others of the means of climbing up after him. In this lies the secret of the cosmopolitan doctrines of Adam Smith, and the cosmopolitan tendencies of his great contemporary William Pitt, and all his successors in the British government administrations.
>
> Any nation, which by means of protective duties and restrictions on navigation has raised her manufacturing power and her navigation to such a degree of development that no other nation can sustain free competition with her, can do nothing wiser than to throw away these ladders of her greatness, to preach to other nations the benefits of free trade, and to declare in penitent tones that she has hitherto wandered in the paths of error, and has now for the first time succeeded in discovering the truth.[69]

The Development of Economic Institutions

In Chapter 2, I described the four types of institutions which the state needs to develop, in addition to its macroeconomic responsibilities, if it wants to increase its economic growth

---

69   Friedrich List, *The National System of Political Economy*, Longmans, Green & Co., 1985.

rate. These are the institutions underpinning its markets, its system of corporate governance, its national system of innovation and its education and training system.

In neo-liberal political economy, there is a global best set of institutions which all governments should adopt. These institutions include, for example, a developed stock market with an easy merger and acquisitions regime, a flexible labour market and a shareholder-oriented corporate governance system. To the extent that these do not exist, it is due to the presence of an intrusive and excessively bureaucratic state which upholds monopolies, prevents competition and deliberately creates and profits from shortages and bottlenecks.

The political economy put forward in this book, however, and my own personal experience, would suggest that in this area developing countries suffer not from too much government interference but from the failure of governments to develop the institutions appropriate to their stage of economic development. The problem is not that the state is too strong but too weak. The state lacks the capacity to develop the institutions which are necessary for economic growth.

It is also important to understand that there is not a global best set of institutions. If we look at the global standard institutions which are promoted we see that they are neither the institutions used by the highest number of countries nor the ones that most developed countries use. Their use is in fact largely confined to Anglo-American economies, especially the USA. Successful developed countries use a wide variety of institutions, and there is no evidence that the institutions used by Anglo-American countries are superior to others.

It is also not clear that the global standard institutions promoted by Anglo-American countries are suitable for developing countries. For example, the Anglo-American stock market serves mainly as a market for corporate control rather than as a channel for financing new investment. It is likely, therefore, to be far less suitable for a developing country than the presence of a development bank. It is also the case that the Anglo-American countries, when they were developing countries themselves, used very different institutions from the ones they are now advocating. For example, the US heavily regulated foreign investment when it was a net importer of capital.

The debate about the political economy of development is often seen as a battle between the supporters of the Washington Consensus and its opponents, with the World Bank and the International Monetary Fund being strong supporters of the Washington Consensus. But in recent years the World Bank has undergone a gradual evolution towards a more market-institutional perspective on market reform. Its 2002 World Development Report was called 'Building Institutions for Markets',[70] and made many sensible points about the reform of market institutions. But it stopped short of pointing out the need for a strong state to develop and reform a country's

---

70 World Development Report 2002, 'Building Institutions for Markets', World Bank and Oxford University Press.

economic institutions, and for donor countries to focus more of their aid on helping developing countries do so.

National Systems of Innovation in Developing Countries

While the form that economic institutions need to take in developing countries is different from that in developed countries, this is particularly so in the case of national systems of innovation because firms in those countries are operating behind the world's technological frontier. For them, therefore, the process of economic development is one of catch-up. How do their firms acquire the organisational and technological capabilities which firms in developed countries possess?

The fact that they are involved in catch-up means for developing countries that technological advancement will usually involve imitation, reverse engineering, and adoption of capital embodied innovations, learning by doing and learning by using. This is in contrast with firms operating at the world's technological frontiers who seek to grow by means of inventive discovery and patenting.

This seems such an obvious point that it is difficult to see why it is not at the centre of the work of all development economists. However, except for economic historians, development economists as a whole have not paid much attention to the process of catch-up. There are two reasons for this neglect. Firstly, neo-liberal theories of growth have seen the principal reason for low productivity and incomes as being low levels of physical and human capital, as opposed to inadequate access to, or command over, the organisational practices and technologies in advanced countries.

Secondly, the imitation of the organisational practices and technologies in advanced countries is seen to be an easy and costless task if there are no barriers like intellectual property rights. But, of course, the technological learning involved in the process of catching-up is not easy, as technology invariably involves a tacit element, that is, it cannot easily be written down and involves some element of learning-by-doing. Technology cannot simply be taken off the shelf, and putting it to use is not a costless diffusion of perfect information.

The question which, therefore, needs to be asked is whether a study of the national systems of innovation of successful developing countries provides any lessons for policy-makers. I believe that it does, and that there are two elements of the national systems of innovation of successful developing countries from which lessons can be learnt. These lessons concern the cross-border flow of people and the role played by government itself in technology transfer.

If we look at successful examples of catch-up by developing countries one of the most obvious elements of their national systems of innovation is the cross-border flow of people, with some of their citizens going to learn abroad, and then returning, and people from advanced countries coming to the developing country as advisors, and in some cases settling there. Knowledge about British textile manufacturing methods was brought over to the United States by British technicians. The development of Japanese industry in the late nineteenth and early twentieth centuries was helped by the recruitment of foreign professors to work as consultants, and the recruitment of specialised technical personnel to work on specific industrial development projects.

In Taiwan the government also played a significant part in the 1980s in bringing back Taiwanese scientists and engineers who had studied abroad and were pursuing successful technical careers there, particularly in the United States. Measures were taken to attract them back to Taiwan. Facilities were created in the Hsinchu science-based industry park to help them form companies of their own. In selected areas of high-technology, start-up capital was provided by the government. In total 19,000 scientists and engineers returned from abroad between 1950 and 1988, with their families provided with better quality housing and their children going to bilingual schools.

A second important element of national systems of innovation of successful developing countries has been the involvement of the government itself in technology transfer. The actions of governments in this area were usually customised to meet the needs of specific industries and took a number of different forms.

Firstly, there was the diffusion of global technological developments. In Taiwan, Korea and Singapore the successful development of the semiconductor industry depended on the presence of a public sector R&D institute that scanned global technological developments, mastered new techniques, and diffused them to the private sector. In Taiwan the lead agency for electronics was ITRI/ERSO, in Korea it was the Korean Institute for Industrial Economics and Trade, and in Singapore it was the Singapore Institute for Micro-electronics.

Secondly, there was the spinning off of domestic companies. The Taiwanese government not only sought to attract FDI to manufacture products in their country but also sought by negotiating local-content obligations and joint ventures to ensure that the technology was transferred smoothly over time to local firms. To help domestic firms emerge it also spun off firms from ITRI, its industrial research institute and its first laboratory, the Electronics Research Services Organisation (ERSO). ERSO's technical projects typically involved licensing a technology from foreign firms, and then creating a pilot plant to master the technology and provide training for local personnel. Then, at the end of the project, the technology would be transferred to a spin-off firm. So in 1976, ERSO acquired RCA's metal oxide semiconductor technology and diffused the relevant know-how to a spin-off firm, the United Microelectronics Corporation, through a demonstration factory and the transfer of key engineering personnel.

Later in the 1980s ERSO promoted the formation of private spin-off companies by contributing venture capital and technological assistance to researchers who intended to exploit technologies developed or acquired through ERSO. This led to the formation of the Taiwan Semiconductor Manufacturing Corp. (a joint venture with Phillips for VLSI chips manufacture), Taiwan Mask Corporation (fabrication masks), and Vanguard International Semiconductor (DRAM manufacturing).

The third way in which governments became directly involved in technology transfer was in the provision of suitable infrastructure for industrial clusters. This was the case in the formation of all the electronics and semiconductor industries in East Asia. Singapore has the Jurong Science Park, Taiwan has the Hsinchu science-based industry park, and in the 1990s Taiwan extended the park concept to the creation of a multi-story incubator building on the ITRI campus designed to house the operations of new technology-intensive firms, most of which were formed by ITRI personnel.

These technology transfers initiatives involved in some cases 'picking winners'. But these efforts should be clearly distinguished from similar efforts of more advanced countries. For 'fast followers' such as Taiwan the technologies they acquired had already been developed elsewhere and were in commercial production. The governments did not, therefore, have to take the risks associated with new technologies. A country like Taiwan also became very good at ensuring that measures aimed at building capability were balanced by measures to curb wealth appropriation and inertia. All incentives offered were performance-based. If a company was given a tax credit for its export performance, then its tax credit would be discontinued if it failed to achieve its export targets. Also there were no bailouts for companies that failed.

Successful developing countries also built research establishments focused on the needs of industry. As early as 1900 the

Japanese government established an Industrial Experiment Laboratory to conduct testing and analyses on a contract basis for national firms, and in 1916 supported the founding of the Iron and Steel Institute of Japan, which diffused technological information among its members through publications, seminars and the work of its Co-operative Research Divisions, launched in 1926 as a mechanism for organising collaborative research.

In South Korea there was the founding of the Korea Institute of Science and Technology (KIST) in 1966, to carry out contract research for industry and government along the lines of the Batelle Institute in the US. In the early 1970s, there was also the founding of the Korea Advanced Institute of Science (KAIS) as a specialised institution offering graduate level education in science and engineering focused on the emerging needs of industrial development. The 1970s also saw the creation in Taiwan of a number of research institutes including the Institute for Information Industry (III) and the Industrial Technology Research Institute (ITRI).

Finally, the concept of national systems of innovation is usually used when industrial development is being considered. But it is equally relevant for the development of agriculture, with the emphasis being on research and extension services, that is, technical support by people who understand not only the technologies but also variations in climate and soil conditions.

This is an important point because agriculture in poor countries is usually the place where they need first to raise their productivity, and also because it is probably in agriculture that neo-liberal economic policies have been most harmful.

Neo-liberalism does recognise the problems that arise if the market mechanism is relied on for the generation and diffusion of new technologies in agriculture. However, it doesn't believe that these market failures are serious enough to justify state intervention, and has, therefore, strongly promoted the involvement of the private sector.

Moreover, while not specifically recommending cuts in research and extension services, the political reality is that when a government is put under pressure to cut budgets, the cuts inevitably fall on weak ministries such as agriculture, and on expenditure such as research and extension services whose harmful effects are not immediately obvious.

It should also be noted that here, as in the protection of infant industries, the policies promoted by particularly the USA and the UK are in total conflict with the policies that they pursued when they were trying to raise the agricultural productivity of their countries. In both cases there was a major focus on public research and extension services.

Late Industrialisation

I now want to look at whether the ideas that I have put forward in this chapter about the role of national systems of innovation in developing countries explain the economic performance of the group of countries that industrialised after the Second World War, and is, therefore, validated by what they achieved.[71] With decolonisation in Africa, Asia and the Middle East a group of

---

71   Alice H. Amsden, *The Rise of 'the Rest'*, Oxford University Press, 2001.

Third World countries with pre-war manufacturing experience, mostly in Japan's 'East Asian Co-Prosperity Sphere', managed to break into world markets, increasingly producing and selling higher-value-added products. In 1965 these countries supplied less than one twentieth of the world's manufacturing output, but by 1995 they supplied nearly one fifth. It was an extraordinary achievement, and it owed very little to the neo-liberal policies which for most of the period they were urged to adopt.

The first point to note about these countries, which consisted of China, India, Indonesia, South Korea, Malaysia, Taiwan and Thailand in Asia, Argentina, Brazil, Chile and Mexico in Latin America, and Turkey in the Middle East, is that they had all acquired some pre-war experience manufacturing silk, cotton textiles, foodstuffs and light consumer goods. They knew something about production and project execution. Their managers had a working knowledge of accounting and finance, and understood the socially complex institution which is the firm. This was an essential platform for their later industrialisation.

The source of this manufacturing experience differed, however, among these countries. India, China and Turkey were all former empires with manufacturing going a long way back in time. India and China had also under imperial rule developed modern textile mills, owned by Indian and Chinese nationals and based on foreign technology transfer. Turkey's know-how on the other hand came partly from Europeans who had lived in the Middle East for centuries. Brazil, Chile and Mexico had acquired know-how from emigrés and later foreign firms.

But while they had some manufacturing experience these

countries did not initially have the organisational and technological capabilities to compete against developed countries in
free markets. Countries such as Korea and Taiwan in the early
years could only sell products such as plywood and wigs made
from human hair, and in the textile industry, even with the low
wages of their female workers, they could not compete in the
1960s against the highly successful Japanese textile industry.

To compete their textile companies required better machinery, more experience in mixing raw cotton and setting the
speeds and feeds of equipment, more ability to switch rapidly
to manufacture the types of yarn and fabrics that came into
vogue in different parts of the world, and more market information. Without these capabilities, which took more time and
resources than most entrepreneurs on their own could afford,
countries such as Korea and Taiwan could not match Japan's
high productivity, and we find that developed countries often
remained leaders in such labour-intensive products long after
their comparative advantage in low wages had disappeared.

In the face of such an inability to compete, and also often a
balance of payments deficit due to local demand for new exciting products such as air conditioning, sewing machines, and cars
and trucks, the late industrialising countries began in the 1960s
to create the development policies and institutions they needed.
They had to find a way to take advantage of their low wages, and
acquire the organisational and technological skills they needed
to move up the ladder of comparative advantage from low-tech to
mid-tech industries like steel, cement, chemicals, rubber,
glass, shipbuilding, machinery and automobiles, and finally into

mature, high-tech products when these were outsourced to developing countries in order to lower their costs.

The late industrialisation countries adopted three sets of policies in order to help their firms upgrade their products. Firstly, they instituted a period of import substitution followed by one of export promotion, in order to help their infant industries compete in world markets. Secondly, they sought to create a significant number of professionally managed, large-scale, national firms. And, thirdly, after a period in which they imported their technology, they began to do their own R&D.

As part of a policy of import substitution to build up their national companies so that they could compete, governments provided their state-owned enterprises (SOEs) and private-owned enterprises (POEs) with tariffs and cheap finance in order to build up their organisational and technological capabilities before they were exposed to trade liberalisation. Exporting turned out to be too tough a first step for firms lacking the necessary organisational and technological capabilities. So they were first subsidised to build up their capabilities, and only then given incentives to export.

But very importantly governments also took action to prevent their economic interventions leading to corruption, abuse and inefficiency. To minimise these problems, they built up a complex set of institutions that amounted to a control system. These attached performance standards to the subsidies, tariffs, entry restrictions and cheap credit that governments allocated to pioneering enterprises. In the same way that developed countries gave innovators patents as an incentive and a reward, developing countries gave firms protection and other financial aids to build up their businesses. But if the government gave a firm a financial incentive, the firms had to give something back to government in exchange, such as reaching an export target, an output level, an investment rate, or a management practice. Development banks such as Brazil's BNDES also subjected their clients to monitorable standards.

A classic example of a country following this development path, and moving from being a low-tech country to being a high-tech one is South Korea. To modernise its textile industry in the 1950s it closed its markets to foreign exporters, including the most competitive of them all, Japan. It also stopped Japanese textile companies from acquiring Korean textile companies. It then set out to acquire the organisational and technological capabilities it needed. A major source of know-how was its British and Japanese textile machinery suppliers. Independent Japanese textile engineers were also hired as consultants, and the Korean government created a graduate engineering major in textiles at Seoul National University, which was modelled along the lines of Tokyo's National University. The import substitution phase of the 1960s gave the *chaebol* the opportunity to develop the manufacturing skills which enabled them to become the efficient consumer electronic parts and component assemblers of the 1970s.

The second set of policies that the late industrialisation countries adopted in order to help their firms upgrade their products focused on the need to create professionally managed, large scale, national firms. The more successful countries understood clearly that if they were to build up their organisational and technological capabilities it would have to be done by its own national firms because the level of a country's investment in skills is very much influenced by the mix of its business structures by size and ownership (private or public, foreign or national). The strategic decision of firms to 'make' or 'buy' technology is also a function of the same factors. And it appeared that multinational enterprises didn't invest locally, especially outside the North Atlantic, in the same types of advanced skills as they invested in at home.

The task of creating professionally managed, large-scale, national firms was greatly eased in East Asia by Japan's wartime disintegration. Korea and Taiwan temporarily lost their strongest foreign competitor and also inherited Japan's banking and manufacturing properties. Indonesia appropriated Dutch assets in the 1950s, and Malaysia began to take over British agency houses soon thereafter. Many British agency houses in India had divested their holdings following independence, and Indian investors triumphed over foreign investors frightened by the political changes.

The retaking of the domestic market in Latin America was not so easy. It benefited from Britain's wartime dislocation, but at the same time it had to confront a powerful northern neighbour strengthened politically and economically by war. Not only did Latin America not experience the same breakdown in foreign ownership that Asia experienced but many of its existing national enterprises were acquired by new foreign firms. In Mexico, for example, about 50 per cent of foreign investments in the early post-war years are estimated to have taken the form of takeovers of national firms.

It should also be noted that where new national leaders were created in the late industrialising countries they tended to be a product of government promotion. In the case of the private firm it was likely to be either an affiliate of a diversified business group with a history of government patronage or a state spin-off. A state spin-off could take many forms, involving more or less government support: a joint venture between the government and a foreign technology leader, a 'model factory' with a mixture of state, foreign and private national ownership, a defence-related contractor that benefited from dual-use technology transfers, a privately owned enterprise 'crowded in' by a SOE as observed in downstream petrochemical industries such as synthetic fibres; or a small firm spun out of a public research institute.

The third set of policies involved support for R&D. In the initial stages all late industrialising countries imported technology rather than generating it themselves. The technology flows that soared after the Second World War made late industrialisation possible. Before the 1990s at the earliest, it is difficult to identify any major industry that developed in the late industrialising countries without foreign know-how.

Measured as the sum of total world receipts of royalties and fees (mostly for foreign licences), developed countries' exports of capital goods, and technical assistance to developing countries, technology transactions rose from roughly $22 billion in 1962 to $356 billion in 1982. This was a thirteen-fold increase compared with only a threefold rise in the unit value index of all manufactures exported to developed countries over the same period. The role of governments in developing countries during this early period was mainly focused on getting the best terms for technology transfers and slowly increasing investments in R&D.

But gradually over the years some countries began to invest heavily in generating their own technology, a necessary condition of sustainable national enterprise. If we take the figures for R&D spending set out in the table below, we can see that Korea and Taiwan were the big R&D spenders. By the 1990s the share of R&D in their GNP had become comparable to that of North Atlantic countries and Japan. Then came India and Chile, whose R&D spending was almost totally natural resource-oriented, followed by Brazil, Turkey and China. The figures for R&D expenditures of India and China were low but still impressive in the light of the vast size of their agricultural sectors, as agriculture was a large component of their GNP but generates a small amount of R&D spending. As the manufacturing activity of Malaysia, Indonesia and Thailand was small it is not surprising that their R&D spending was low. The low spending of Argentina and Mexico on R&D should, however, be noted. In view of their relatively advanced manufacturing sectors at the time of the Second World War their investments in R&D spending fifty years later were very small. In case anyone thinks that these figures are of no significance industrially it should be pointed out that the cumulative number of US registered design and utility patents in 1995 was 32 in Argentina, 60 in Brazil, 1,240 in Korea and 2,087 in Taiwan, and the growth rate between 1980 and 1995 was lower in Argentina than in any other late industrialising country except Mexico.

Table 8.2 Research and Development Expenditure, Selected Countries, 1985 and 1995

R&D Expenditure (% of GNP)

Country	1985	1995
Korea	1.8	2.8
Taiwan	1.2	1.8
India	0.9	0.8
Chile	0.5	0.7
Brazil	0.7	0.6
Turkey	0.6	0.6
China	n/a	0.5
Argentina	0.4	0.4
Malaysia	n/a	0.4
Indonesia	0.3	0.1
Thailand	0.3	0.1
Mexico	0.2	0.0

(Viotti, Eduardo B. (2001), National Learning Systems: A new approach on technical change in late industrializing economies and evidences from the case of Brazil and South Korea. Technology and Innovation Discussion Paper No.12, Center for International Development, Harvard University.)

A major reason why Latin America grew more slowly than the United States and Canada over the years is the market-directing institutions which the Spanish conquistadors introduced into Latin America to exploit the native population. But this story also has a modern chapter because if we go back to the 1950s the prospects for growth in Latin America seemed more favourable than those of Asia. American investment in Latin America was substantial, and the levels of industrialisation, as measured by the ratio of manufacturing to agricultural net product, and the net value per head of population, were well above those in Asia. Argentina was seen as being almost 'developed' or industrialised.

However, by 1970, the four tigers of East Asia, South Korea, Singapore, Hong Kong and Taiwan, were generally being put in the same category as Brazil, Mexico and Venezuela as Newly Industrialising Countries (NICs). Then in the 1980s there was a very sharp process of differentiation between the Latin American NICs and the East Asia NICs. The East Asian countries continued their rapid growth and even accelerated it, while the Latin American countries slowed down or declined. As we saw at the start of this chapter real GDP growth rates per cent p.a. per capita were negative in the 1980s in sub-Saharan Africa and Latin America, but rose quite fast in South Asia and very rapidly in East Asia.

This divergent performance between the two areas has to be seen as a process story. If we consider the initial conditions of the two areas in 1950 as their initial 'endowments', then these 'original endowments' cannot be used to explain their different growth rates. Looking at the industrial structures, education levels and availability of natural resources in Latin

America in the 1950s, neo-liberal economic thinking would have forecast higher growth in Latin America than in East Asia.

However, the concept of national systems of innovation can be used to explain the divergent performance between the two areas, and in particular the distinction made by Eduardo Viotti between 'active' and 'passive' learning systems can be used, as he does, to explain the difference between the performance of two countries typical of their regions, South Korea and Brazil.[72]

In his analysis of the two countries Eduardo Viotti argues that there are two forms of technological absorption. There is first of all technological absorption that requires the minimum technological effort, such as turnkey projects, licence agreements and foreign direct investment. This enables a firm to do little more than produce goods and services, and can be seen as 'passive' learning.

The second form of learning requires much more of a technological effort and takes the form of imitation and reverse engineering. This leads to a deeper mastering of the absorbed technologies and, therefore, to a richer array of opportunities for active incremental innovation. This he describes as 'active learning'.

He then goes on to argue that passive learning is the most common form of firms' technological strategies in

72   Eduardo B. Viotti (2001), 'National Learning Systems: A new approach on technical change in late industrialising economies and evidence from the cases of Brazil and South Korea', *Science, Technology and Innovation Discussion* Paper No. 12, Centre for International Development, Harvard University.

developing countries. Also active learning only takes place where there are the right external institutional conditions which encourage the deliberate, aggressive accumulation of technological knowledge, and which take a social rather than a private perspective on the returns to that accumulation. The simple functioning of market incentives is likely to favour a passive learning strategy in late industrialising economies, and an active learning strategy requires a more complex set of institutions, relationships and incentives.

Finally, Eduardo Viotti produces a mass of indicators under three headings to show why South Korea was successful in the transition to an active learning system whereas Brazil was not. These indicators he organises under three headings: their national patterns of education and training of their labour forces; their national patterns of technology acquisition; and their national patterns of commitment of resources to technological learning. I find these indicators very persuasive and I have listed the key ones in Table 8.3. He also includes indicators on the outcome of the national technological effort which I also find persuasive and have summarised in Table 8.4.

Table 8.3 National Learning Systems – Brazil and South Korea Selected Input Indicators

	Brazil	South Korea
Labour Force Education and Training		
Adult illiteracy (1995)	16.7	2.0

% of age group in secondary education	43	93
% of age group in tertiary education	11.5	48.2
% of first university degrees in engineering	7	18

Technology Acquisition

Imports of capital goods as a ratio of Gross Domestic Investment	0.259	1.066
Foreign direct investment up to 1986	US$ 27.4 bn	US$3.6 bn
Direct purchase of technology	US$827.8 m (1984–88)	US$1,517 m (1982–86)

Technological Effort

Expenditure on R&D as a percentage of GNP	0.4 (1994)	2.1 (1992)
Expenditure on R&D by source of funds		
- Government	81.9	17.2
- Productive enterprise	18.1	82.4
- Other	-	0.4
	(1994)	(1992)
Scientists and engineers engaged in R&D (per million inhabitants)	235 (1993)	1,990 (1992)

Researchers according
to place of activity %

- Government	26.16	17.40
- Universities	68.51	33.15
- Private sector	5.33	49.46
	(1986)	(1987)

(Viotti, Eduardo B. (2001), Ibid.)

Table 8.4 National Learning Systems – Brazil and South Korea Selected Outcome Indicators

Patents	Brazil	South Korea
Patents granted by the national bureau to residents (1991)	14%	69%
US patents granted to residents in each country (1993)	57	779

Trade in high tech products with the U.S.

	Brazil	South Korea
Exports of advanced technology products (1994) (US$ million)	115.8	6,658.4

Diffusion of new productive technologies

	Brazil	South Korea
Robots per million in employment	52 (1987)	1,060 (1987)
CAD (Computer aid design work stations) per million in employment	422 (1987)	1,437 (1986)

| NCMT (numerically controlled machine tools) per million in employment | 2,298 (1987) | 5,176 (1985) |

(Viotti, Eduardo B. (2001). Ibid.)

National systems of innovation in the broad sense that I have used the concept in this book clearly interact with other features of a country's social and political systems. For example, land reform in Japan and South Korea, and the Communist Revolution in China, have meant that the opposition to social change of a traditional land-owning class has not in East Asia been the major problem it has been in Latin America. Nevertheless, the figures that I have quoted in this chapter make it very clear, I believe, that the speed and success of a developing country's industrialisation depends critically on its national system of innovation as well as the effective functioning of its other economic institutions.

The Role of the State

This review of the economic performance of successfully industrialising developing countries makes it clear, I hope, that the state has a key role to play in ensuring that its economic institutions work efficiently, and in particular in developing the institutions which enable and incentivise firms to accumulate organisational and technological capabilities. If the state develops the right institutions its firms will be encouraged to upgrade the organisational and technological levels of their operations. If the state makes the wrong decisions, its firms are likely to remain stuck as lowest-cost producers.

These technological institutions, as we have already seen, can be R&D institutes that can scan global technological developments, quickly master new techniques, and diffuse them to the private sector. They can also be institutions like Taiwan's Industrial Development Bureau and Singapore's Economic Board which target industries which on the basis of good technical advice and analysis can feasibly be developed. Other institutions that one finds are development banks or investment vehicles such as the China Development Corporation in Taiwan, institutions to attract investment such as Singapore's Economic Development Board, institutions for export promotion such as Korea's Trade Investment Promotion Agency, and trade associations such as the Taiwan Electrical and Electronics Manufacturers Association which provide a means for communication between government and firms, and a way of reaching consensus over new directions for an industry.

To set up and run such institutions clearly involves considerable skills, but because of the widespread belief in neo-liberal ideas, development economists have not taken much interest in these institutions, and developed countries have given developing countries very little aid to help set them up. As Tony Blair has pointed out, the development community seems to be much more worried about the developing countries doing wrong than 'the challenge of getting things done'.[73] The major donor countries of the OECD invest more than $3.5 billion in governance

---

73 'Not Just Aid – How Making Government Work can Transform Africa', speech by Tony Blair, hosted by the Centre for Global Development in Washington, DC, on 16 December 2010.

every year, but much of this, perhaps as much as 60 per cent, is spent on what are essentially attempts to tackle corruption. This involves supporting public financial management systems and strengthening civil society, oversight bodies, parliaments, media, NGOs, human rights watchdogs and anti-corruption commissions. The fight against corruption is clearly very important, but the question has to be asked as to whether some of this money could not have been better spent on strengthening their capacity to develop their economic institutions.

It is, of course, the case that government policies to upgrade industries can easily lead to corruption and wealth appropriation. A system of incentives designed to encourage firms to move into new economic activities can easily become a means by which businessmen and bureaucrats enrich themselves at the expense of the community. It is wrong, however, for politicians and policy-makers to respond to this problem by seeking to insulate public officials from businessmen as this will have a detrimental effect on the essential flow of information between them. A better way to tackle the problem is the system of performance standards which successful developing countries have used.

It is also very important that any support given for capacity development is targeted on what the government involved sees as the barriers to them achieving their top policy priorities. As Tony Blair had said, capacity building programmes 'can't succeed unless they have the backing of political leaders, and they won't get that backing unless leaders can see a clear link to the things that they most care about: delivering tangible results that citizens will notice'.

As a result of my experience in East Africa I believe that a much higher proportion of capacity building funds should be directed at helping countries build up their capability to do such things as develop sound agricultural policies, put in basic infrastructure such as the supply of electricity and negotiate with foreign companies who are seeking to develop the country's natural resources.

To anyone who is an objective observer of developing countries the importance of having an active and competent government is obvious. If we look, for example, at post-war South Korea, we see a strong centralised state with a well-functioning national bureaucracy. Its relatively high administrative capacity is partly the result of the small size of the country but also probably a result of Japanese control and colonisation in the period 1905 to 1945, and the imposition of Japanese bureaucratic structures.

In this respect Taiwan also probably benefited from Japanese rule from 1895–1945, in the same way that Hong Kong and Singapore acquired effective administrative structures as British colonies. Obviously the acquisition of administrative skills does not in any way justify either Japanese or British colonialism, but it does provide a partial explanation of why they were able to develop faster than other countries.

In this chapter and previous chapters I have described the enabling role the state needs to play if a high level of economic growth and fairness is to be achieved. But to perform such a role successfully the state needs to be made more capable, and to be protected from the demands of special interest groups, and how this can be done is the subject of the last chapter.

NINE

THE ENABLING STATE

A major failure of Progressive politicians and policy-makers in the past thirty-five years has been to allow the role of the state to be denigrated and ridiculed by neo-liberals. They have also done very little to reform it and make it fit for purpose in the twenty-first century. And when Progressive politicians and policy-makers have come to the defence of the state they have left people confused as to whether they are defending the role of the state or public sector employees.

A first task of Progressive politicians and policy-makers in the twenty-first century is, therefore, to persuade people of the importance of a competent and active government, standing above sectional interests, both for economic growth and the quality of their lives. Without a competent and active government Progressive politics can achieve very little, and the key question which has to be answered is not the size of the government, but how it can best define and uphold the public interest, and how it can be reformed so that it has the capability to do so in a cost-effective way.

251

The Role of the State

The role of the state described in this book, however, is a different one both from the command-and-control role advocated by traditional socialists and the minimalist role advocated by neo-liberals. It is an enabling role, and should be seen as a market-supporting one rather than a market-directing one. It is not the role of government to do what private enterprise should do. As J. M. Keynes said:

> The most important Agenda of the State relate not to those activities which private individuals are already fulfilling, but to those functions which fall outside the sphere of the individual, to those decisions which are made by no one if the state does not make them. The important thing for government is not to do things which individuals are doing already, and to do them a little better or a little worse; but to do those things which at present are not done at all.

This idea of the Enabling State is based on two key observations. Firstly, economic history over the last fifty years has taught us very clearly the importance of private initiative and incentives. An examination of economic development demonstrates clearly that it is the collective result of individual decisions of entrepreneurs to invest in risky new ventures and experiment with new ways of doing things. Even left-wing economists now have a healthy respect for the power of market forces and private initiative.

At the same time, as has been shown a number of times

252

in this book, the economic conditions in a country have an important influence on the strategy and performance of firms in it. As Michael Porter has written:

> Competitive advantage is created and sustained through a highly localised process. Differences in national economic structures, values, cultures, institutions and histories contribute profoundly to competitive success. The role of the home nation seems to be as strong as or stronger than ever. While globalisation of competition might appear to make the nation less important, instead it seems to make it more so. With fewer impediments to trade to shelter uncompetitive domestic firms and industries, the home nation takes on growing significance because it is the source of the skills and technology that underpin competitive advantage.[74]

Thomas Friedman has argued that we live in a flat world and that advanced ICT technologies now mean that knowledge pools and resources have become connected all over the world, levelling the playing field and making each of us potentially an equal competitor of everyone else. If this means that markets are increasingly global, and that it is easier for most people in the world to access information, then it is unarguable. But if it means that everyone has an equal opportunity to be innovative and compete on equal terms with other people around the world, then it is demonstrably not true. 'In a flat

---

74   M. Porter, *The Competitive Advantage of Nations*, New York, Macmillan, 1990.

world,' Friedman writes 'you can innovate without having to emigrate', but for many people that still is not the case.[75]

As Richard Florida has pointed out, both population and economic activity are heavily concentrated at particular points across the world, and innovation is even more concentrated. The world of innovation is a spiky world not a flat one.[76]

If we take the patents granted in the United States, which are generally accepted as a good indicator of patent activity around the world, then we find that nearly 90,000 of the 170,000 patents granted in the United States in 2002 went to Americans. Some 35,000 went to Japanese inventors and 11,000 to Germans. The next ten countries including European countries, Taiwan, South Korea, Israel and Canada produced 25,000 more, and the rest of the flat world produced just 5 per cent. Also in 2003 the University of California produced more patents than India and China combined.

These figures do not show that Indians and Chinese are not innovative, but that they had to travel to places like Silicon Valley to translate their creative ideas into products and businesses. Annalee Saxenian, of the University of California Berkeley, has shown that Indian and Chinese entrepreneurs founded or co-founded roughly 30 per cent of all Silicon Valley start-ups in the late 1990s.

These figures also illustrate one of the paradoxes of globalisation, which is that geography has become both less and

---

75   Thomas L. Friedman, *The World is Flat*, Penguin Books, 2005.
76   Richard Florida, 'The World is Spiky', *The Atlantic Monthly*, October 2005.

more important. High-tech firms can now locate their operations wherever they wish in the world. But if they want to be competitive they need to locate their innovative activities in knowledge and information-rich regions where there is a concentration of ideas, talent and risk capital.[77] These figures also demonstrate the importance of national systems of innovation, and why governments should seek to make them as effective as possible.

The growth of globalisation in recent years has led many business leaders, economists and politicians to argue that it is not possible today for the state to play any role in economic affairs. To support this point of view they argue that countries are now part of an integrated world market which has stripped nation-states of virtually all powers, and has forced them, in order to earn market confidence and attract trade and capital inflows, to adopt policies of tight money, small government, low taxes, flexible labour legislation, deregulation and privatisation. What Thomas Friedman has called the 'Golden Straightjacket'.

If developed Western economics were involved in a 'race to the bottom', and if there was nothing that governments could do to create the conditions that firms need to innovate and grow, then these arguments would be compelling. But, as we have seen, developed Western economies are involved in a 'race to the top', and the state has a key role to

---

77 Adam Segall, 'Is America Losing Its Competitive Edge?', *Foreign Affairs*, November/December 2004.

play in designing and reforming its country's institutions; its financial and labour markets, its system of corporate governance, its national system of innovation and its education and training system.

What I am advocating in this book is also very different from the failed 'industrial policies' of the past. It is not about trying to control the corporate strategies of firms but about creating the best possible conditions for industry to innovate and grow.

In looking at what role we want the state to perform we need to keep in mind a number of key points so that we don't repeat the mistakes of the past. Firstly, as has been argued throughout this book, it is ultimately a nation's firms that create and sustain the competitive advantage that enables them to be successful in the global marketplace. Governments can shape and influence the institutions that surround firms and the technologies available to them but they should not get drawn into shadow corporate decision-making. Even when aided by the best civil servants, governments will make foolish decisions about the corporate strategies that a company should adopt, or the products it should develop, as governments cannot be as knowledgeable about market forces or corporate strengths and weaknesses as corporate executives can, nor can they always prevent their decisions being distorted by political forces.

Secondly, the role of government towards a nation's industry is to stimulate the dynamism and upgrading necessary for success in the global marketplace. If competitive advantage is seen as driven largely by factor costs, government may seek to lower these costs, and thus reduce the pressure on firms in an industry to innovate and change. Government policies should always, therefore, be measured in terms of their effects on the dynamism and long-term productivity growth of the firms they involve. If this is done the chances of them hindering economic growth rather than accelerating it will be greatly reduced.

Thirdly, competitive advantage is created through a long process of upgrading human skills and investing in key new technologies. This is an area where government can play a role, but it should involve industry in determining what skills are created and in which technologies it invests. The key resources are specialised, and need to be aligned with the emerging needs of industry, and government should bring firms into the decision-making process, and also encourage them to play a major role themselves in creating such resources.

Fourthly, the best conditions for industry to innovate and grow is neither a quick nor necessarily a popular course of action. Most of the best levers for creating the necessary change are slow-acting ones such as creating advanced skills, investing in research, encouraging competition and using demand to stimulate innovation. As a whole, most firms and workers would prefer quick and undemanding solutions such as subsidy, protection and boosts to domestic demand. However, if politicians can isolate their decisions from the political power of special interest groups and adopt the policies recommended in this book, then they can help create a world in which there is faster economic growth and greater social justice.

Finally, in the last thirty years neo-liberal economists have promoted the idea that regulation of economic activity by government is unnecessary, futile and a major burden on industry. As a result regulators have been encouraged to take 'a light touch' approach and there have been major failures of regulation, particularly of financial markets. This attitude needs to change. We should not forget that regulatory failure was a major cause of the financial crash of 2008.

We need to stop the endless flow of trivial regulations produced by Parliament, and make sure that the regulations which do exist are cost-effective and up-to-date. But once that is done, we need to make certain that they are effectively implemented by the regulators. We need to return to a world where people can run their businesses and trade, knowing that the risk of such activities has been reduced because the government has laid down, and will enforce, rules and regulations for the conduct of economic activity. We need to return to a world where the effective and efficient regulation of economic activity is seen as an important function of government, and where regulators are seen to be doing a useful job. It is an essential feature of 'the Enabling State' that government is seen to be helping people fulfill their ambitions and is not seen simply as a burden on them.

The Capability of Government
It is not enough, however, for politicians and policy-makers

to decide on what is the best role for government; they must also make certain that it has the capability to carry out the tasks that it has been given, and that it is protected from the special interest groups who want to frustrate its efforts to uphold the public interest. If the argument is accepted that the state can and should play an important enabling role in the economy, then if it fails to do so it should be reformed and not simply allowed to abandon its duties.

I have argued in this book that there are four areas of economic policy – in addition to its macroeconomic responsibilities – where the state has a key role to play in designing and reforming its country's institutions: its financial and labour markets, its system of corporate governance, its national system of innovation and its education and training system.

It is also important that responsibility for these four policy areas is clearly allocated to the relevant departments of government, that processes are put in place to co-ordinate them and that the capability of the relevant departments is built up so that they can carry out these responsibilities effectively. There is no reason why civil servants and politicians can't carry out these responsibilities effectively but they need to have the skills and experience to do so, and the necessary organisational processes also need to be in place.

What this means in practice can once again be explored by looking at the situation of the UK government. As far as the allocation of responsibilities is concerned, responsibility for analysing, monitoring and, if necessary, reforming the way the financial markets work is something that should clearly be allocated to the Treasury. An advantage of science policy being handled by the Department of Business, Innovation and Skills, and not as in the past by other departments such as the Department of Education, is that it means that the Department of Business, Innovation and Skills is well placed to manage the national system of innovation. In addition it should also have responsibility for corporate governance. The Department of Education clearly should have responsibility for the education and training of the nation's workforce, and the Department of Work and Pensions should be responsible for the efficient functioning of the labour market.

There is also a need for a committee or council at the centre of government to co-ordinate the work of the different departments, and to make certain that the four key policy areas that I have described get the attention they deserve. In setting up such a committee or council, a future government would do well to look at the National Economic Council (NEC) which was created by Prime Minister Gordon Brown in response to the economic crisis of 2007/8.[78]

This institutional innovation is generally regarded as having been a success. It joined up departments, it speeded up decision-making and delivery, and it secured collective buy-in to its positions. While the major fiscal and monetary decisions, allied to the behaviour of employers, were the main

---

78 D. Corry, 'Power at the Centre: is the National Economic Council a Model for a New Way of Organising Things?', *The Political Quarterly*, Vol. 82, No. 3, July–September 2011.

reasons why the early stages of the recession were less painful than they might have been, the NEC made a major contribution through measures such as help to the young unemployed and the longer term unemployed, help for school leavers not only when they leave in September, but also in January for those still without anything; support for business through the Time to Pay schemes (that allowed deferral of tax, VAT and National Insurance contributions), through business lending schemes and help for trade credit insurance; help for the car industry through the scrappage scheme; support to the house-building industry through kick-start and shared equity products; and support to regeneration schemes that were in danger of collapsing.

Three factors seem to have been important for the success of the National Economic Council. First it had the strong support of the Prime Minister who was willing not only to give time to chairing the meetings but also to be fully engaged in their preparation and process. Secondly, the Treasury was prepared to cede some of its authority over economic policy thinking. A great weakness of the UK system of governance is that the Treasury fights hard to keep other departments out of economic policy. Thirdly, there was the role played by the NEC Secretariat, driven by the Cabinet Office, which reports to the Cabinet Secretary.

While in the UK the centre of government is usually regarded by the media and commentators as being over-powerful, the tools that it has for driving the government machine are indirect, largely bilateral and thinly spread.

The NEC managed to break down the silos of government through a strong Prime Minister, an activist secretariat and collective high-level support. Unfortunately, the coalition government has not continued with the NEC, though it has created a mechanism for securing more collective action on the national security side. A future government which wanted to drive forward a major reform of the UK's economic institutions would do well to look at creating a similar institution to the NEC in order to achieve its goals.

Finally, there is a great need to improve the efficiency of government in the UK, and I suspect in many other countries as well. While there has been a huge amount of debate about the size of government there have been only sporadic and half-hearted efforts to improve its efficiency. As a result both politicians and civil servants are asked to operate a very dysfunctional system, and this inevitably leads to a huge amount of frustration and endless recriminations.

There are four areas in particular where I believe significant changes need to be made. The first is the lack of clarity about what is the responsibility of ministers and what is the responsibility of civil servants. In the UK constitutionally everything is the responsibility of the Minister other than the Permanent Secretary's role in seeing that the money which is allocated to his or her department is spent properly. But no one really believes that ministers have the time, or in most cases the knowledge and experience, to manage their departments, and as a result when there is a major management failure in a department no one is clearly held responsible.

A second systemic problem is the lack of anyone with the constitutional responsibility for managing the Civil Service. I had naively thought when I became a minister that the Head of the Civil Service was like the CEO of a company and had the job of managing it. But I gradually realised that the Head of the Civil Service has no authority over the Permanent Secretaries who head the various departments, and that the UK Civil Service is best described as a loose federation. Politicians often ask why government policies are not better joined up, why the monitoring of the performance of departments is so poor, and why so little action is taken in response to the management failures of departments. The answer is simple. No one has the responsibility or authority for seeing that these things are done.

Thirdly, while it is generally claimed that the policy-making process of the UK Civil Service is of a very high quality, there is no evidence to show that this is the case, and the process by which policies are developed appears to be very amateur. There are virtually no policy units to collect information, work with external research organisations, review what is happening in other countries and regularly review policies. Policy reviews are largely ad hoc, and carried out by individuals who don't necessarily have any training in policy-making or any relevant knowledge or experience.

Finally, over the years various tasks have been delegated to a variety of so-called non-departmental public bodies. But because these have been set up at times when there were very different views as to what roles they should play, and because they perform very different functions, it is almost impossible to say what responsibility a minister has for NDPBs in his area. This quite predictably leads to a low level of performance.

There is also a need for a more intelligent debate about the outsourcing of the functions of government. This is an issue which is usually debated in ideological terms, with right-wing politicians arguing that it is always desirable because private industry is always more efficient than governments, while left-wing politicians, except in recent years, have usually argued that it is undesirable because the profit motive is not a good way of incentivising people carrying out public functions. But there has been little debate about how outsourcing increases the capability of governments, and which functions it is effective and efficient for governments to outsource, and which it is not.

It is, however, possible to lay down four criteria which in government – as in business – need to be met, if outsourcing is to be successful. First, it must be possible to measure easily the output of the outsourced function, and, therefore, determine whether the function is being performed well or badly. If it is not possible to do so easily, the firm to whom the function is outsourced will simply cut costs, perform the function badly, and make more profits, or alternatively the government will have to spend large sums of money monitoring the firm's performance. Secondly, there must be a number of firms with the necessary skills who want to perform the function, because if there are not, government won't get the benefits of competition.

Thirdly, it is essential that neither lengthy experience nor corporate memory are of importance in carrying out the function, because, if they are, in a world in which there are frequent competitions to carry out a function the performance of firms will be poor. Finally, the outsourcing of a function will not be successful if the performance of the function has to be closely integrated with other activities of government and, therefore, constantly changed and developed in complicated ways, as it is impossible to write such changes and developments into a contract in an efficient and effective way.

Applying these criteria it is easy to see why it makes sense, for example, to outsource the catering facilities of government departments. It is easy to measure their performance, there is plenty of competition, neither experience of government nor corporate memory are of great importance in carrying out the function, and the requirements of government departments don't change frequently or in complicated ways.

On the other hand, the idea that policy-making can be outsourced, as proposed recently by the UK coalition government, fails at least three of these criteria. It would be very difficult, for example, to say whether a management consultancy has developed a good policy to deal with youth unemployment or not; experience and knowledge of previous policies would seem to be essential, and the development of a policy for youth unemployment should be an interactive process involving the minister, and carefully integrated with other government policies. There might be a number of organisations who would want to compete for such a contract, but how many of them would have the necessary skills is debatable.

This is not to say that policy-makers in government should not draw on the knowledge and resources of research institutes which work in their policy areas, and there may be occasions when it is useful to get them to challenge the policies put forward by civil servants. Such steps would seem to be a useful part of any carefully constructed policy-making process, but it is not the same as the outsourcing of a government function.

It may be said that these are all boring constitutional and organisational issues and that what is required is more leadership. But if you want a high-performing organisation which is good at policy-making and implementation, which is innovative and which has citizen-friendly services and a good control of capital and revenue costs, these are issues that need to be resolved.

Defining and Upholding the Public Interest

I see the primary role of government as defining and upholding the public interest. In the last thirty years of market fundamentalism the idea that there is such a thing as the public interest has been allowed to atrophy. But I believe that it is an idea that needs to be revived.

If governments, however, are to stand up for the public interest successfully, a first requirement is that they are able to resist the financial power of interest groups. At the beginning of the twentieth century the US President Teddy Roosevelt declared that 'the supreme political task in our day is to drive the special interests out of our public life'. And, today, that still must remain a key task of government.

Political parties play an essential role in a country's democracy. They produce the leaders for whom electors vote at elections and they develop policies. It is, therefore, vitally important that political parties obtain the funding they need in ways that do not expose them to the suspicion that donors are able to receive favours or improper influence in return.

It is possible once again to look at what needs to be done by analysing the situation in the UK, where current arrangements fall far short of what they should be. The public are highly sceptical of the motives of both donors and recipients. This is not surprising as all three main parties depend for their funding on a relatively small number of individuals, trade unions or other organisations, and all require their leaders to spend time soliciting more money from these sources. This has produced an unending stream of scandals, which cannot be good for democracy.

In November 2011, the Committee on Standards in Public Life produced a report 'Political Party Finance – Ending the big donor culture', which sought to remedy the situation and make it more truly democratic. They made four key recommendations which build on what happens in other democratic countries. Firstly, a limit of £10,000 should be placed on donations from any individual or organisation in any year to any political party. Secondly, the cap should apply to donations from all individuals and organisations, including trade unions, though they point out that if individual trade unionists were required to opt into paying affiliation fees, then these could be paid to political parties. Thirdly, the existing limits on campaign spending in the period before an election should be cut by the order of 15 per cent.

Finally, they argue that existing public support to political parties should be supplemented by the addition of a new form of public support paid to every political party. This should depend on the number of votes secured in the previous election, at a rate of around £3.00 a vote in Westminster elections and £1.50 a vote in devolved and European elections.

The Committee is at great pains to point out that they would not recommend a public subsidy to political parties if they thought there was an alternative, and that the cost of the additional support might amount in total to around £23 million a year – or fifty pence a year for each UK elector. This seems to be a small price to pay for cleaning up party funding.

I support the proposals of the Committee because of my lengthy experience of political party funding. I made donations in the UK to the Social Democratic Party for many years to keep it afloat because I thought a new political party was needed in British politics. I have also given large sums to the Labour Party in recent years both because I don't think that general elections should be won because one party has a huge financial advantage over the others, unless this is broadly based on popular support, and because I think that the Labour Party should not be solely funded by the trade unions any more than the Conservative party should largely be funded by financial interests.

However, I believe that the current system of party funding is totally unsatisfactory. The trade unions have only to say that a particular issue is of importance to their members, or for investment managers and bankers to say that a particular issue is of importance to them, for Labour and Conservative ministers to feel that they must take action, knowing that in a general election they will be very dependent on these groups for funds.

At the time of writing this book it is not clear whether the three main parties will come to an agreement to take the committe's proposals forward, though all three in their last election manifestos said that they would seek to reform party funding. They are concerned that they might be put at a disadvantage, though the Committee on Public Standards seems to have produced a fair solution.

The electorate needs to insist that action is taken. An innovative and dynamic economy requires the guidance of an enthusiastic and involved democracy, and an active and competent government which is capable of carrying out the tasks it is given and able to stand up to the financial power of interest groups. In the UK we are rightly proud of our democratic traditions. We could be prouder if we took action to reform them in the light of the current danger they face.

We Can Choose Our Future

In all developed Western countries we face today a major economic challenge. How does the state create the conditions that enable firms to upgrade and move into higher-value-added products and services? If the state in a country does so, then I believe that country can look forward to a future of economic growth, exciting and dynamic cities, and attractive job opportunities for young people. If the state in a country doesn't, then I believe that country will be condemned to a future of stagnant living standards, urban decay and high youth unemployment. The current economic crisis requires political leadership of a high order. Politicians need to rethink their political and economic ideas and persuade the electorate to change their views, but I am convinced that if political leaders and political parties adopt the political economy of Progressive capitalism, then they will gain the support and win the votes of the people of their country.

Capitalism is not a form of spontaneous order or the embodiment of a structure of basic human rights, but one of the great constructions of the human mind. It is a set of institutions which must be justified by its contribution to the well-being of society, and as such should be perpetually open to reform. There is no one best set of institutions which all countries should adopt, and a country's institutions need to be reformed constantly to meet the challenges of a changing world. Capitalism should not be seen, therefore, as a static concept but as a perpetual work in progress.

Neo-liberals will tell people that they have no choice but to submit to the harsh realities of an economic system which cannot be changed. It is the job of Progressive politicians and policy-makers to tell people that there is plenty of room for choice. The economic policy space of countries is larger than is commonly thought, and we can build a better society combining economic growth, liberty and social justice if we have the desire and will to do so.

270

ACKNOWLEDGEMENTS

This book has benefited enormously from endless discussions and critical comments from many people, including Andrew Adonis, David Halpern, Will Hutton, John Kay, Roger Liddle, Ira Magaziner, Peter Readman, Peter Riddell, Andres Velasco and Paul Wooley. I also owe an intellectual debt to Ha-Joon Chang, who introduced me to the concept of institutional political economy.

John Coatsworth, the Provost of Columbia University in New York, has given me invaluable support over the long period it has taken me to write the book. He also put me in touch with a number of his colleagues who gave me a great deal of help and advice. In particular Miguel Urquiola made many useful comments on the whole book.

I would like to thank the two government Chief Scientific Advisors, Lord May and Sir David King, and the two Director Generals of the Research Councils, Sir John Taylor and Sir Keith O'Nions, who taught me a great deal about science and innovation while I was in government.

Finally, I would like to thank my editor Sam Carter, my agent Andrew Wylie, my secretary Jane de Brûle, and my Political Advisor Joe Burns for all their enthusiastic help, and for making the production of this book an enjoyable experience.

INDEX